BUGGIN' OUT

A.J. SCHMITZ

MAXIXAM
PRESS

Copyright © 2022 A.J. Schmitz
All rights reserved

Registered with Library of Congress - U.S. Copyright Office

First Edition

ISBN: 978-0-578-35752-2

Cover design and interior book layout by A.J. Schmitz
Cover photo by Maximilian Schmitz

View A.J.'s work at: ajschmitzdesign.com

For Rita and Maximilian.

Sorry for being such a pain in the ass.

Everything in this book is true.

Some of the names have been changed
to protect the guilty.

CONTENTS

Introduction	The Benefits of Self-Publishing	1
1	Tree Wishes and Death Wishes	11
2	Buggin' Out	25
3	The Dog Days of Summer	35
4	Rah-Rah, Sis Boom Bah!	59
5	30 Years and Counting...	71
6	To Quebec and Bec Again	87
7	Condiments, Conditioners and Coffee	99
8	Footlocker Treasures: Part I	113
9	Microwaves and Diamond Rings	127
10	Food, Glorious Food!	141
11	Generation X, Y and Z	149
12	Buggin' 2 - Electric Bugaboo	165
13	Footlocker Treasures: Part II - The Sequel	179
14	Candy Flipping with The Dead	195
15	Cult of Personality	209
16	Footlocker Treasures: Part III - In 3D	221

INTRODUCTION

THE BENEFITS OF SELF-PUBLISHING

In the mid-2000s, I wrote a book called *One Foot In The Gutter*.

You've never heard of it.

It's a heart-pounding masterpiece about a New York private eye named Emilio Josepy. A recovering drunk, he gives his life a reboot and moves to Los Angeles to try his hand at screenwriting. His only vice, besides working out, is sticking his nose in other people's business. He gets involved with the hottest girl at the gym and before he knows it, he's investigating an illegal chemical dumping scheme that is poisoning the local waters.

It's a brilliant novel. I like to think of it as a modern take on *Chinatown*, filtered through *Leaving Las Vegas*... except funny. A guaranteed beach-reading staple.

If not destined to become a fixture atop the *New York Times* Best Sellers list, then surely atop the Christmas lists of every bookworm over the course of many, many years.

I shopped the thing around, hoping an agent would see its immediate allure and agree to stick it under the noses of the finest book publishers in the land.

But the response, let's just say, was underwhelming.

Then, a friend had a friend, who had a book agent shopping *her* book, so she would speak to him about me. To my surprise, I got a phone call a few days later from a book agent named Jonathon Lazear. Couldn't tell you one thing we said to each other on that call, but I sent him my manuscript.

And to my utter shock, he loved it!

Jonathon and I sized each other up on a warm spring day at a café near his apartment on the Upper East Side of Manhattan. Jonathon was a big doughy guy, about 55-ish, with a head like a ripe, carve-able pumpkin. When we shook hands, his paw swallowed my bony fingers in what appeared to be warm, plump sausages.

We squeezed into chairs around a tiny European-styled wrought-iron table and sipped espressos. Like the character of my book, Jonathon was a recent transplant himself, having moved from Minnesota to New York after his divorce. About the subject of his break-up, his air teetered between regret and relief. There were kids, almost grown, but I assumed he was like millions of people on the planet who simply outgrew their old married life and was starting anew.

We discussed some loose terms of a contract --10% of something -- and perhaps, we traded beaver pelts and a knife. I'm not positive. A firm, meaty handshake was in there to be sure. We parted ways and that was that.

Basically, I went back to my apartment in the East Village and counted the days until the major book presses banged down my door with complicated, multi-book contracts.

Before long, letters of rejection filtered in from publishers. Jonathon would open the letters, read them, stuff the letters into envelopes and mail them to me downtown.

"This is an interesting story, but I hate the protagonist," dripped one.

"There's some interesting things happening in this book, but I don't like the prose," smacked another.

"I like the narration, but the story is a little unfocused and not believable."

This went on through about eight, heart-spiking notices.

With each letter, I would rethink the myriad ways I would change the story to improve it, until the next rejection letter came and countered everything the other publisher had just said.

Learning quickly that you can't please everyone -- or anyone, really -- I called Jonathon to get his thoughts. He seemed genuinely miffed by the rejections. During the course of the conversation though, I revealed that I had already written a sequel to *One Foot In The Gutter* called *One Foot in the Door*. In this follow-up masterpiece, our hapless hero Emilio stumbles into a black-market organ-trading ring.

I sent the sequel to Jonathon and, to my great shock, he liked it more than the first book! So, Jonathon decided to change course and shop *Door* instead of *Gutter*. Within days, I started getting rejections of that book.

"Fascinating story, but the writing is just so-so."

"I love the interaction of Emilio and Detective

Dupree, but there's a lot of problems with this book."

And then, of course, there's the old hand grenade, "This just isn't for us."

After a few months, Jonathon decided on a new plan of attack. How the new attack would differ from the old attack, I couldn't say. I did have a third book in the works, *One Foot in the Grave*, but that wasn't remotely finished. That third book involved Emilio getting involved with a serial killer. The idea of throwing another book into the mix not only seemed unfocused, but downright reckless. Whatever plan of attack we needed to reconsider probably involved nothing more than me smoking weed in my apartment while he sent more manuscripts to other publishers.

I definitely wasn't going to *rewrite* the books because, as I stated before, they were brilliant.

Besides, I was too busy writing speeches for the cartloads of book prizes I'd be winning, as well the acceptance speech for the Oscar I'd be awarded for Best Adapted Screenplay.

Focused on important stuff: Who would I be thanking at the Oscars? Should I tell a joke first or simply state how hard I've been working? I'll look stunned, of course, then feign confusion as to why I was chosen over more worthy candidates.

But how long should I wait till I look into the camera to tell all the downtrodden viewers in their depressing homes to "Never give up on your dreams?" The scenarios were endless.

On a bright summer afternoon, I met Jonathon at his

apartment on 86th street between First and Second avenues. It was a Spanish-style building well-shaded by a large, leafy sidewalk maple. Jonathon's apartment was sub-street level, with a small sliding back door to a postage stamp yard, something pretty rare for Manhattan.

His place was bursting with sunlight, the opposite of my East Village cargo container hovel. Over a tall glass of vodka-spiked lemonade, we sat and chatted. From what I recall, the yammering focused very little on the new book blitzkrieg other than hitting some smaller publishers and focusing on *One Foot In The Door*, which he felt was more fleshed-out, better written and scarier. I felt that *Door* needed *Gutter* to familiarize the reader with Emilio and Detective Dupree, but I relented. He was the expert.

Suddenly, I got a strange sensation…almost a combination of the planets aligning and what one might describe as the panic tinge of food poisoning. Just as my stomach rolled, Jonathon drastically changed the topic of conversation from literature, to one about the mental and physical benefits of having one's asshole massaged.

That was quickly followed by the pop question, "Have you ever had your prostate milked?"

In the moment I couldn't tell you how I felt about the conversation. I was dizzy to be sure. Unsettled, most definitely.

Being a heterosexual male, I would've been flattered if the question had been posed by, say, Brad Pitt -- or maybe even George W. Bush. But Jonathon was more like the Stay-Puft marshmallow man from *Ghostbusters*, only with a mop of sandy grey hair parting from his crown like a Boston fern.

Perhaps this all seems shallow, as if I would have succumbed to his poisonous whims if he'd been handsomer and his fingers not similar in girth to steaming bratwursts. But if I was inclined to switch teams in the middle of a game, the choice would more likely be for the team's dashing star second baseman -- and not the goofy, overstuffed mascot.

Looking at the bottom of my nearly finished lemonade drink, I found a sediment that I assumed was a poor ratio of Country Time lemonade mix to cheap vodka, but pegged as some sort of half-assed, kitchen sink roofie. The smell of the chemicals not only rolled in my gut, but perforated my sinuses like Vicks VapoRub. I excused myself to use the bathroom. Unfortunately the only facility was the one next to his bedroom. As I passed Jonathon's dresser, I noticed a display of Magnum condoms fanned across the top like a Vegas croupier might do with a deck of playing cards before screwing you out of all your hard-earned money. The gold-foiled cock covers were so glistening, and the intent so apparent, you'd have to be blind not to notice.

I entered the bathroom, lifted the toilet seat and emptied my gut in the most seamlessly way possible. I was an experienced drinker who'd hurled his guts more than a few times in my day, but this was akin to tossing a pitcher of water out the window. Plop! Out and done. I exited the bathroom to find Jonathon eclipsing the sun in the door jamb of his shaded bedroom.

He asked if I was OK -- then proceeded to massage my shoulders. For some reason I let him. Probably because it prevented me from falling over and crashing into the condom dresser—my vision narrowing like a carriage horse. Jonathon continued his discourse on prostate massaging, telling me that a doctor had recently performed this procedure on him and the release he had was "life-changing."

Now, I'm not on the board of any medical institutes, nor do I work for the federal or local government, but if your doctor is giving you prostate massages, there's a strong chance your doctor is doubling as a prostitute or you've accidentally wandered onto the set of a pornographic film titled *Dr. Strange Glove.*

I was trying to control my nausea, veering in and out of clarity until I felt one of Jonathon's sausage fingers stroke my asshole, which perked me up to a soldier-at-attention level of awareness.

I collected myself, thanked him for the lemonade and headed out the door. He stood sheepishly at the apartment door and watched as I squinted and poked at the wall for elevator buttons. Since he was sub-level, the hallway was crime-scene dark, yet I finally discovered a cool metal button-like object on the wall. As if guided by spirits, I was in the lobby passing brown Spanish bricks and arched doorways until I was back on 86th street in the blinding light of the sun as it fell towards Hell's Kitchen on the west side.

Then, like waking from a dream, I was completely conscious and alive. What saved me, I decided, was that I was an experienced drug taker and booze drinker. Someone of a lesser constitution may have collapsed and fallen under the weight of Jonathon's cocktail concoction. I had built a tolerance so high that having walked just a few blocks, my body processed the roofie from brain-clobbering date rape drug to energy drink. I then completed a brisk, 77-block walk down First Avenue to my apartment on 9th Street in the East Village.

As you might imagine, I didn't talk to Jonathon after that. Embarrassed, but mostly dejected, I let everything just fade away. I filed no police reports, made no calls or accusations, and he offered no apologies. The rejection notices stopped coming in the mail, the books got shelved, and I moved on with my creative life in other frustrating and satisfying ways.

Once I finished writing *Buggin' Out*, I began the arduous task of finding a book agent. Today, with most processes done through the internet, the rejections were swifter, and yet, no less painful.

If you've ever lost your job, you know that looking for a new job becomes a job in itself. You evaluate yourself as to why you are a worthy and valuable human being, which leads to piles of self-doubt and hourly humility checks. Same goes for writing a book. You write a book and not only do you spend massive amounts of time trying to find an agent who may like it and try to sell it, you spend countless soul-crushing hours telling those people why you are talented, which you'd hope the book itself would do for you. But it's a velvet rope scenario. To have the book read, your cover letter needs to be razor-sharp and explain why your book is good (without saying it's good), in the shortest way possible, until your letter of introduction registers you as an unqualified moron who should be lumped together with every non-talented dope that's ever written a book from here to Timbuktu in the last 100 years.

INTRODUCTION

Not only that, if you do get someone to appreciate your work, there's the potential chance they're a lunatic who likes prostate massages or perhaps, some other kind of perversion. That's too great a risk to venture into the murky waters of the shark-infested agent world. Don't get me wrong. This isn't meant to shed a bad light on book agents. All fine people I'm sure -- prostate focused or not. Nor is this to frown on prostate massages... or any kind of massage. In fact, if we're speaking truths, I'm up for just about any sexual excursion, as long as I'm conscious. So, let's just say, I'm a touch gun shy these days. My anxiety about this book rose before an agent even entered the picture.

The second half of the process, shopping the book to publishing houses, is even more daunting. They're all looking for the next big thing and that is most likely *not* me. I'm not sure I have the power to convince them otherwise whether it be via cover letter, email, phone call or even over stiff lemonade drinks at a fancy hotel restaurant or a tiny espresso cafe.

So, because of this wonderful invention called the internet, I've decided to skip past the agent *and* publisher portion of this process and venture into the world of self-publishing...along with about eight billion other people. This will pretty much guarantee that no one will read this book other than a handful of people I beg to buy it on social media.

Enjoy.

BUGGIN' OUT

1

WISH TREES
AND DEATH WISHES

It was Spring... creeping up on Summer. I was feeling completely unanchored and lost in life. Drifting aimlessly day after day, on my feet and in my thoughts, through the streets of Manhattan. I'd just moved out of my friend Mark's apartment on 69th street when he decided to return from North Carolina after a failed attempt to live the life of an antiques dealer. He'd purchased an unruly ancient home down there, filled it with cardboard boxes and proceeded to brick himself in like a man walling his own mausoleum. Multiple Sclerosis had crippled him, and his last resort was to die in Manhattan – a place where you could at least shuffle to McDonalds to get coffee and if you fell, someone might be polite enough to drag you to your apartment.

Mark's real name was Joe, but he changed it to Mark because Joe felt like an average name to him. Average Joe. Growing up in conservative Sacramento, Mark was, as he'd often say, an out-of-place queer trying to find himself in the world. At fourteen, his mother put a gun to her head and emptied the contents of her skull onto the kitchen wall – an act that tortured him deeply for the rest of his life.

By eighteen, Mark was living in Manhattan. As if abandoning his conservative Christian family for hedonistic New York City was not enough of an insult to them, he was an identical twin, and changing his name had crushed his family – his twin brother most of all.

While baking in the sun on a rock in Mexico, Mark was discovered by a talent agent who found him fetching. He modeled clothes and cigarettes in fashionable magazine ads. He looked like the mustached Marlboro Man, so the work was plenty. On his adventures through the streets of Marrakesh and the frenzied bazaars of the world, he became a collector of seductive, shiny things. Tangible artifacts that made his mind swirl with child-like wonder.

I'd been six months single after escaping a relationship with a woman who was already married -- to three cats -- an animal I'm deathly allergic to. She introduced me to Mark and we became fast friends. He was twenty years my senior, but we bonded over being collectors with an appreciation of the craftsmanship of history's relics. He fancied silver, silks and pearls. I admired comic books, vintage video games and toys.

Over the years, I've known more Marks than any other named person. In college, I was in a band called *The Jays* where every member but myself was named Mark. I attract Marks. And Marcs. I attracted this Mark through the cosmic universe as well.

I'd spent four years planted inside the cushy lair of Mark's rent-controlled apartment while he toiled away down south. I grinded hard, day and night, to build a career and make a name for myself in the marketing and advertising world. But when Mark returned, I was forced out into the cruel world of reality where rents were higher and the dating pool lower. I'd moved ten blocks up 1st avenue to 78th Street, spending my evenings wandering home after work in the humid spring nights, waiting for the invisible ghost of life to sweep me up to some secret party. Where the cool people were... or something like that. Weird fantasy, I know. Wouldn't it be great if someone spotted your amazing coolness and dragged you around the city on a perpetual party tour? I was up for anything.

I worked at HBO, which sounds sexy as hell if you're making fabulous TV shows about city whores, gangsters of the Jersey shore or dragon queens of lore. But if you're anything but a producer in the building, you're another monkey working for the grinder man. But like most buildings, there were people. Good people. Some of them friends.

One of those people was Chihiro Nishihara. She was Japanese. One day she told me of a special event.

"A party?" I beamed.

No. A blue moon. Blue moons are rare; but rarer still are full blue moons. And even rarer is when they fall on the summer equinox, which Chihiro assured me was a time of great rejoice in Japan. All these events were about to align that very day. Passing by her office, she must have smelled my desperation and divulged this info to me like a nurse dispensing pills to a patient. "This one's for your blood; and this one's for your heart..." Her info *was* for the heart. And the hopeless.

Which may have been me. Probably me. Definitely was me. She told me that on the evening of the Equinox, people in Japan make a wish, write it on paper and hang it in a tree.

That night, I stopped by a bar named Bounce, a high-class Hooters where the girls were 25% hotter and the drinks 50% more expensive. No one I knew was there, so I bellied up to the bar and drank alone. The bartender was polite and when I asked for some paper; she fished around and gave me a yellow sticky note pad. I told her about the Equinox-wish tree thing, so she tried to write one herself.

Of course, in Japan, when they do something of this nature, it's glorious. They write on ancient parchments faded from time with inks bled from mashed flower pedals and hang them in blooming trees with colorful ribbons that sway in the wind, while woodwind instruments whistle lullabies in the sky. I had a yellow Post-It note and a rubber band and it was good enough.

I sketched through some early wishes: millionaire, crazy famous, artist of outstanding renown, prolific filmmaker and animator. All of them seemed flat and desperate, which they were. If the Genie pops from the lamp and offers you three wishes, you go for the good stuff. Money is easy. Fame is stupid, but desirable for the lazy and vain. Fame? Sure, international love! You have so much to offer, shouldn't you be loved like Picasso, Einstein, Hitler...Why not be crazy famous? But when it came down to it, I simply wrote "I want true love." Tragically romantic. Stupid even. A wasted wish some might say. But in the moment, completely desirable to me. More than fame or fortune - a companion. Later that night I went to the tree outside my apartment building and hung the

Post-It wish on a branch and went to bed.

Passing the note bouncing on its rubber lanyard the next morning, I pranced to work with what one may describe as a 'demeanor of magnetism' or in New York City parlance, not staring at the sidewalk.

But nothing happened. No flood of people, no parade of lovers… nothing. I worked all day and returned home that night. The wish was still there, hanging naked in the tree. Accessible for anyone to rip down, toss it, stomp on it… use it against me in a court of law. And the next day came and went too with nary a single person of interest coming from the woodworks.

Incredulous, I stormed Chihiro's office the next morning, ready to mock an entire country for false wish-fulfilment fantasies. Apparently, she forgot to mention an important part of the process. The need to *burn* the wish. I raced home that evening, snatched the wish from the tree and burned it in the kitchen sink with a lighter.

The next night, coming home from work, to my surprise, I saw something under the tree where I placed my wish. It was a woman. Small, beautiful, dark-haired and exotic brown eyes. Just my type. I scrambled upstairs and dropped my briefcase, then bounded back down the stairs like a gazelle and introduced myself.

She was Brazilian, unanchored and lost too. She'd come to New York to find another path. After running herself into the ground managing her town's most popular luncheonette, she took a calmer office clerk job, and was let go after only a few months. An acquaintance offered her a nanny job in Manhattan and now she was here. I asked her to come have a drink with me and she did. Along the way I asked her name. "Heata" she said. Heata? I repeated it like a dummy. Living in New York I'd heard a lot of names, but not Heata.

Although Manhattan is stuffed, overflowing actually, with amazing restaurants and bars, I took her to a bar named American Trash around the corner... so named because of its collection of unwanted furniture, games and wall signs of other bars. Bad name... good bar. She barely spoke a lick of English. Using bar napkins, we doodled hieroglyphics to communicate. I sketched a computer to indicate I was a designer and she drew a baby to indicate being a nanny. She wrote her name.

Rita. Ahhhh, Rita. Now I get it! I realized later that Brazilians pronounce their R's like H's.

We drank a beer and I kissed her within the first 20 minutes. I drew a picture of a fish on a plate with a fork and knife -- my invitation to have dinner at a nearby seafood place the next night. Returning home, we realized that we lived across the hallway from each other. A direct line of sight to blow kisses to one another.

I knocked on her door the next evening. I was invited inside by the couple who'd brought her there for the nanny position. Larissa, who was with child, and Sando, a jazz guitarist who wore sunglasses regardless of the time of day. Fellow Brazilians. As we departed, hand in hand, into the evening, I assured them I'd watch over Rita very carefully.

Rita looked stunning. She wore painted-on jeans and a white top. I wore a smile. A doorman breathed envy as I walked by with her on my arm. We hit a seafood place called Aqua-something. It had a fish above the main door. We ate tuna and drank beer. I was armed with a little rice-paper notebook from Chinatown – rescued from my junk drawer. During our dinner, we continued to fight through the language barriers. I drew a picture of a film projecting an image of a house being lifted by balloons as my invitation to see the Pixar film, *UP*.

She nodded and the next day we were at the movies.

The dating continued on and on... and two months after we met, she got pregnant. We dove in with both feet. She moved into my tiny apartment that was barely big enough for one person, let alone three. We got married at the Louis J. Lefkowitz marriage bureau at City Hall the day after Thanksgiving. Coming to Manhattan with the expectation of roast turkey and a tour the city, my cousin Grace got chicken and became a witness to a marriage.

After winter broke and Spring sprung up, we took a short stroll to Lenox Hill hospital where we waited, for what seemed like a month, for our baby to enter the world. For some reason, we couldn't get the guy out. Maybe he was stubborn. Maybe the whacked anesthesiologist, who I swear on a stack of sedatives was as high as a kite, over-medicated Rita to the point of her being crippled below the waist. The second he stuck the epidural needle in her lower spine, she got a fever, and it all went cuckoo from there.

More curious doctors popped in to see what was happening between Rita's legs than in a Times Square peep show. Less people show up in a football huddle than in the congregation of medical staff that gathered to ponder the top of my crowning kid. Eventually, the chief doc called for a C-section and at a click before midnight, our son Maximilian arrived. As purple as a prune with a raging fever himself, I wheeled Max to the newborn NICU center to recover from his jaundice, and left Rita passed out in a medical papoose to sleep it off.

•••

    Two years flew by in the blink of an eye. Rita, Max and I moved to 80th and York. In a whirlwind career-ladder climb, I went from HBO to The History Channel to the Creative Director of a political advertising PR firm. If you thought politicians were stupid sitting from the comfort of your couch, imagine meeting them in person. They do nothing to dispel the notion they're incompetent morons. Some of our clients could barely form sentences, and the ones who could, did so with a level of deficiency that would shock and awe you -- making political PR firms not just an option, but pretty much a requirement.
    I worked 14 hours days for an entire summer, building creative, multi-lingual campaigns for soulless politicians around the 5 boroughs of New York. English, Chinese, Korean and Spanish swirled around my head in a dialect soup while I desperately tried to retain Portuguese in my home, my wife's native tongue.
    Rita was in and out of rehab for Pelvic Floor Dysfunction, a condition where your lower abdomen muscles are strained - usually from childbirth. She'd pushed so much trying to shoot Max out, she'd misaligned her entire body and needed to get an overhaul.
    Rita took a job at a Brazillian school, which often re-

quired her to schlep a gaggle of toddlers through the screaming traffic of midtown. The school was so poorly run, the city threatened to shut it down multiple times. One day a child wandered off on a field trip in Central Park, later to be found by a random guy in an Elmo costume, who may have been anyone from a hard-up teen pedophile to a serial killer fresh out of jail. Taking Max to a job on a daily 2nd avenue bus downtown, packed like sardines with inconsiderate commuters through constant construction to a school mired in violations, nearly drove Rita to the brink of sanity.

Between work chaos, a sleepless baby, medical problems and living on the 79th street bus route that bombarded us with a skull-rattling *vroom* every 15 minutes, our nerves were absolutely shot.

Then, I lost my job and the world came to a grinding halt. A job hunt replaced work and our rent went from difficult to impossible. The savings dried up faster than a sneeze in the Sahara, and we found ourselves unanchored and drifting aimlessly.

Along the crazed journey of work and family, I lost touch with Mark. So I picked up the phone.

When Mark told me he spurned a million dollar offer to sell his collectibles to Martha Stewart, only the limits of technology kept me from reaching through the phone to strangle him. I figured I could wrap a rope around his neck when I saw him, but by the time I got there, I was only mildly annoyed.

"I love my things; I spent a lifetime collecting them," he said.

I knew the reason. I'd seen it a million times over the years. Handing me his fancy pen collection one day, he asked me to sell the glistening scribblers on eBay. But as he plucked each one back, gently massaging them in his fingers as he recollected the stories of their procurement, I left his place empty handed.

'You can't take it with you' was a philosophy I tried to instill, but it fell on deaf ears, the only part of his body that functioned correctly. By then, the right side of his body had completely stopped working. The MS made him legally blind and unable to walk without two canes. Never knowing he'd be using them himself; they were two gorgeous, intricately carved wooden canes he'd gathered on his worldly adventures -- but two canes, none-the-less. A full-time nurse became his roommate, and when she had to start wiping his ass, his dejection dropped from sour to rotten.

Rita and I had just settled on the idea of leaving Manhattan when I got the call. Mark was in a psycho ward. He'd called his nurse a Nazi cunt and threatened to kill himself, which is a trigger word sure to land you in the loony bin posthaste. When I arrived, he was in a strait jacket, pinned to a hospital bed like Hannibal Lecter. The shades were drawn in glowing slots and the room was so sparse, I thought he'd fallen into an abandoned elevator shaft. He'd aged about four years in a matter of days. Tufts of hair fell out, and on occasion, a fingernail dropped off his finger. He was literally falling apart.

Leaning over him, he whispered in a battered voice "I just want to die. I just want to die." I begged him to keep quiet or he'd remain in the god-forsaken cell for the rest of his days. He knew I was right. He drank their soup and kept himself straight. His attitude was temporarily positive with no mention of suicide, yet, we were treading the line of dark territory.

Then it went from bad to worse.

"The surgery went well, but the recovery is going to be very difficult," the surgeon said.

Two days prior to that phone call with the surgeon, another inmate had escaped their restraints and was tearing through the ward like a running back. He blasted into a nurse, she pinballed into Mark, and the three went crashing to the floor in a pile. The nurse trampolined on top of Mark and crushed his hips. He never took another step. It was the beginning of the end.

Mark recovered at home, but his strength and his bank account were quickly draining. He began to lose his mind and thought people were robbing him, which may have been true. The nurses were stealing his Oxycodone, the only relief for his extreme pain.

The state assigned Mark mental health advisors, but there was no point; he was nearly gone physically and mentally. A tattered, gangly mess of bones and skin, he looked like a ghost from a Dickens novel - like something dredged from a lake and propped into an upright position. Bed sores took over.

Having reconnected with his twin brother, his family dragged him to Sacramento where they stuck him in a back room so he could die with kin. But all the reasons he'd left in the first place came flooding back: the Christian zealotry, the screaming heterosexuality, and the heaping spoonfuls of loving hospitality. He'd lived alone for 45 years and wasn't about to be a bird in a cage. After three months, he demanded to go home and the return plane trip surely took more years off his life.

Ms. Stewart's million wasn't the only offer that Mark had declined over time. Since Mark was living in the rent-controlled apartment, the building owners were dying to get rid of him. He'd been there 30-something years and his rent was an eye-popping $120. They offered him $100,000 to leave and he scoffed in their face. He wanted a quarter million, so they scoffed in his face. Both sides decided to dig their heels in and wait. It looked as though management had won this one.

Even though Mark kept saying he wanted to die, I never thought he really meant it. He was blind, crippled and broke to the point of being a negative, but he had a lust for life. A sparkle that never waned and a true love for the possessions he acquired when he traipsed through the world. But by the end, he'd truly meant his words. Not only was he a shell of himself, he was a shell of a human. A brain in a skeleton.

Larissa and Sandro cashed out to quieter Queens with their daughter Victoria. Our friends Ned and Jen bounced with their baby boy Atticus to Brooklyn. And although Max loved buses and dropping plush toys on the heads of unsuspecting pedestrians from his bedroom window, Rita and I escaped with him to the luscious lawns of Long Island.

Not long after that crushing fall in the psych ward, Mark was gone. The news of Mark's death arrived via text, while I was at my new job, from his friend who was with him in the end. I asked for more details, but was made to feel like I was not part of the process -- that perhaps, I'd abandoned him or was no true friend at all. Maybe that accusation was my imagination. Maybe it was true and I hadn't helped Mark enough. I was a new husband and father – not a caretaker to man who continually made the decision to let his belongings bury him both physically and financially.

He couldn't take it with him, but he had all of it while he was here.

In the end I received no further communication about Mark. No invitations to a wake. No funeral notices. No plans for the body and no utterances of final words or wishes. I received no mementos -- none of his collectibles, trinkets or toys. I said goodbye to an old life as I held a new one in my hand. And when I'm asked to lead a prayer at Thanksgiving, I think of Mark, and thank the invisible ghosts of life for good health, because I actually mean it.

BUGGIN' OUT

2

BUGGIN' OUT

I'm in my dark living room with my wife Rita, my son Maximilian and his best bud, Artturi. The boys are drawing pictures in notepads on the floor. A vicious lightning storm cracks outside, which only minutes before, I'd been running in with a bag of laundry the size of a boulder on my shoulder. It was laundry load number 25,000, with another 25,000 more to go before the exterminators got here in the morning. I'm on the couch with my head in my hands, damp from rain.

It was bed bugs... discovered only a day before. Where did they come from? Was it the trip to Connecticut? That Air BnB? Or was it the spiritual retreat my wife took with Nicoletta so she could reconnect her yin with her yang? Does it matter? They're here now. We must eliminate them!

I'd heard bed bug horror stories before, but now it was happening to us! Everyone seems to have a bed bug story.

"Our friend Janice had bed bugs and... oh, my, God. They were everywhere!"

"What'd she do?" I ask biting my nails to the quick.

"What any sensible person would do... burned her house to the ground."

My finances are in such a delicate balance, if they were a high-wire act, the audience would have gasped at the numbers. But it was safe enough for ONE hit... the potential car alignment our shaky Honda desperately needed. A trip to Quebec we'd been looking forward to for a year. And, God forbid, a hospital visit that required out-of-pocket expense. But it was bed bugs. Mother-sucking bed bugs. Thousands of dollars. Just light it on fire. Gone!

We're in the process of preparing the house to be exterminated... following Bed Bug protocol as told to me over the phone by Donna at No Worries Pest Control. "Dry, on high heat, every shred of material you own down to the freakin' pocket square you found stuffed in the back of your closet that you've not used once because you're not that fancy, and stuff it all into plastic bags and seal them. Empty the closets of shoes, shoe boxes, and all the other crap you've lost over time, and prepare for the SWAT team to blast through the windows and hose the place down with cancer-causing poison." Something like that. All well and good. We're good soldiers. Dedicated to the cause. I'm bounding like a gazelle to the laundromat with giant bags of wrinkled clothes because they have huge dryers. Our rental has a miniscule dryer that gets a quarter full when you toss in the spongy fabric softener sheet.

In the middle of the process, with kids playing on the floor... and me running in the lightning... and the road literally breaking apart from the flash flooding... and the windshield wipers incapable of wiping fast enough for the deluge... and the terrible dinner I bought at the market that was filled with pepper... PEPPER! That terrible black powder... almost as dangerous as gun powder in its nature... and everyone throwing the food in the garbage... and everyone's *still* hungry, including me who's not eaten since basically yesterday....and the time... the race against time... the power goes out!

And we sit in the dark around a camping lamp. It's horrible blue glow so intense and uncozy, it might as well have been a rectal exam. The kids don't like the dark. There isn't an iPad that can hit the wifi for miles! So, we sit. Staring at the wall. The time slowly ticking away. The time, ever so precious in this moment, going down into the sewers like the dirty street water. Minutes pass like hours. It's painful. A wait of a thousand waits. The dryer won't dry. The Laundromat, besides being on the same energy grid as our house, will close within minutes. After a large punch in the face by life, this is a definitive kick in the balls for good measure.

I consider burning the house to the ground, but it's not mine... and I'm not good at lying to insurance people.

"Yea, the Picasso... what a loss. His blue period."

Arthur, his big brown eyes blinking at me for answers under his mop of black hair, is waiting to be picked up by his mother who's stuck on a Long Island Railroad train from Manhattan. On a normal day the train is a soul-crushing, monotonously slow commuter nightmare, but in this furious storm, it reaches horse and carriage levels of hair-pulling tedium. An update text comes from her... pause after each excruciatingly long pause, during the creep of the trains' many stops. Then there's a puddle on the floor. A leak?! Oh, My,

God... NO, not now! Wait... No... no no... Not a leak... No. The ceiling is sound. Roof stable... no burst pipe or flooding. Our son's friend filled his backpack with water. "To clean my toothbrush." he says. It's a baffling moment in the quiet chaos. He's nine mind you, not four. Ice cream fills a void where black pepper and chicken did not. At 11:00, the power comes back on and we resume laundry till we are drained of our vital essence at God knows what hour of the morning.

•••

The next morning I'm sitting in my sun-blasted kitchen feeling like death warmed over. I've awoken at 6:00am to shuffle my family into a zombie breakfast and out the door with Zen our cockatiel to my parent's house so they can spend the day doing nothing while the SWAT team comes to exterminate our invasive insect friends. The appointment window is 8am to 10am... and at 10, they don't show, so I call. I'm informed that I'm mistaken and that my appointment is from 10 to 12. I hit the roof! I insist and complain that my appointment was from 8 to 10 because I scheduled my day around it, but it's of little use. The damage to my schedule is done. My day is shot. And really my week is shot because of the incredible amount of careful planning I hinged on everything running like clockwork. Why would things run like clockwork? They never do, so why'd I think this catastrophe would hit all the check marks *this* time? I curse myself. Even if things ran a little late it'd all work out, but this was *massive* time. In the scheme of history, it's a blip on a fraction of a timeline, but in my carefully constructed house of cards calendar, it collapses.

I call the bug company back with a head full of steam and insist, no *demand* to speak with Alison the owner. She offers a whopping $75 discount for my troubles. She reiterates the bug preparation hand manual to alleviate my concerns, except I'm becoming more unraveled because her bug preparation advice *counters* Donna's bug preparation advice. Donna being the woman who advised me before, but who also confirmed my 8 to10 time slot which got screwed up, so now I'm beginning to melt down. The confusion has my head floating like a helium balloon. There's no one to believe! I call work and tell them to cancel our important meeting with a drug prevention center so I can be here from 10 to 12 to meet the bug guy. I consider drugs at that moment, but it won't help. Not much will. Maybe a few drugs… OxyContin, Klonopin… but I don't have any!

After consulting with my completely irrational self, I panic and call my friend Gary, who mentioned he worked for a bug guy years ago. Within seconds bug guy's foreman is calling me. Pete the foreman. Pete is great… why didn't we just call Pete the first time?! I unload my past few days on Pete like a therapist. I'm ready to scrap the plan and go with Pete. Makes total sense. But Pete can't help.

"I've got a full schedule today." He says with a sympathetic tsk.

Pete's busy. Of course Pete's busy! He has a job! But he tells me he'll answer any questions tonight, which is similar to having a bartender make you a cocktail on a cruise ship that's left the dock without you.

Minutes later 'The Guy' Gary once worked for calls. The main guy. The owner. Coach. His name is Coach because he's an actual basketball coach, so everyone just calls him coach. Good thing he wasn't a butcher or a seismologist. I like to call him therapist two! I unload on him...He tells me Donna and Alison's advice is ALL WRONG. Anxiety is in my throat. Is it possible to die by phone call? But then, scheduled bug guy shows... at 1:30. My rage is now exhaustion because I've not eaten, peppery food or otherwise, in two days. While I'm on the phone with Coach, scheduled bug guy is coming up the steps.

I glance anxiously out the window -- like I do when I wait for the mailman to be a safe distance away so I can go out and get the mail.

Bug guy knocks and I let him in and whisper to Coach that I'll call him back. Then a small ray of sunshine hits my soul. Scheduled bug guy is AWESOME! John, the bug guy, is THE MAN. He's properly weathered... a million miles of wind has grated his tattooed arms like beachwood. With a goatee and bandana do-rag, he may have just stepped out of a Viet Nam Vets parade, I don't know. He probably has Lynyrd Skynyrd on constant rotation. I ask 50 questions and he answers them all... and then some. He tells me it's all going to be ok. I believe him! He must sense my complete unraveling. Everyone in this situation usually is.

"I'm impressed with your prep." He says nodding with one of those approving frown smiles.

We did the job right. I beam with pride. He tells me to trust him when he says he's "seen things you don't want to see."

"Hoarders!" he says with an air of horror.

Things that will make you throw up. I believe him. I

won't frown at the cable dust behind my computer anymore.

He tears the place apart and examines every inch with a flashlight. If anyone's going to find these fuckers, it's this guy! He tells me his life story as he twirls the box spring like a ballerina. He's 60...two kids... New York City cop for 20 years... 3 ex-wives... Irish... former Marine...the list goes on. From the smell I can tell he smokes and he informs me the bug killing poison spray is safe so he doesn't use a mask... like a real man! I assume John will be dead in five years, but he's helping us *today*! I imagine he's got a sweet Harley and hits the beach on the weekends. I love this guy. John is the *actual* therapist—spraying my fears away.

"Don't worry." He chimes through five decades of tobacco lung.

Magically, I don't anymore. I convey my feelings to my wife via text, but she's not as enlightened. Perhaps heart emojis could have expressed it, but then it gets awkward. He's just a bug guy. He tells me bed bugs are *lazy*. They don't travel far for their blood feastings. That's why they hang out in beds and bite people. Now I'm openly scoffing at the bed bugs... the shiftless layabouts! Why don't they go out and get a summer job? Stop dragging *me* down. Even a paper route would get them some pocket money.

He's in and out of the house in 15 minutes. I slip John a 20 as a tip... a fair price for therapy. I promise to review him on Google. It's deserved. He says he's going to spend the 20 on "cervezas" emphasizing the last S as a drawn-out Z, which means he's really going to enjoy those cold-frosted bad boys. I wouldn't have it any other way. I plan on having a six-pack or two myself when this is all over. As he walks away, he calls me 'brother' and grins...tells me to... wait for it... "sleep tight, don't let the bed bugs bite." He had to do it... had to! I know he does. He likes it. It's an appropriate exit for a man in his line of work. I give him that "oooohhhh, you dirty dog" side-glance chuckle and toss out the finger guns. I might have winked. I'm not sure. It's an appropriate farewell for a customer.

•••

I'm the first to get home that evening from work. I open the door and smell the poison. I open windows and air the place out. My father arrives with my wife, son and bird. He says he won't come in. He didn't know we had bed bugs! Which means he and my mother aren't communicating, which should come as no surprise to anyone. They live in the same house, but why would that matter.

"What do you want for dinner? By the way, the kids have bed bugs." Easy right?

Later in the evening, our friend Marge texts us that she wasn't going to the city tomorrow and working from home. She didn't have to drop her son off at our place after all... water-filled backpack or otherwise. She seemed desperate for someone days ago, but now it's not a problem. But it's clear... We're fucking lepers. Bed bug lepers. The unloved... *the unvisited*. It's obvious. Clear as day. We followed her text with a suggestion of a play date for the boys, but that excuse was worse than the first. So, it was met with a thumbs-up emoji from us. Best we could muster in our depressed state. It's just us now. The Three Amigos. Four if you count Zen.

The unwanted... and our house filled with bed bug carcasses.

It's OK. When you have no friends and your family barely comes by, it's easy to detach. Where should we go? California? How about Italy? Tuscany is a place my wife has always wanted to go. Maybe we go to Brazil, my wife's home country. She misses it. Her family misses her. She longs. I don't care. Let's go... In times of trouble, we've swung wildly in thought from living on the other side of the planet to travelling around in a camper. The glory of living on the road a grand idea until you think about things like hot showers and edible food. But, if we're not to be visited... what's to keep us from drifting away?

Bed Bug John had inspired me, but there was another blow. Donna promised I could pay with cash, check or a credit card. Sounded perfect. Except they billed my debit card, overdrawing my bank account. -$11. Pow! Punch in the face, kick in the balls, and now... I'm up against the ropes. And this is the shit that makes you stop and say, "This can't be life!" I thought at this point in my history, I'd be sunning on the Riviera, golden tan, donning a speedo and mirrored sunglasses, hair slicked-back with oil, waiting for a James Bond vixen to dock her wood-hulled Hacker-Craft speed boat on the beach and summon me to her yacht with the clang of crystal champagne flutes. In reality, you hope and pray that you'll be comfortable... money in the bank, a homeowner and able to withstand hard luck situations. Unfortunately, we couldn't muster any of those things. But real life has a habit of getting in the way of your fantasy life. And as you get older, your fantasy life consists of stimulating thoughts like, decent health insurance and tires with treads on them.

A few days later I'm on the computer furiously researching Bed Bugs. Minutes before I'd spotted a dark spot on the floor and was positive it was a filthy bed bug. They're BACK?! It sent me into a terrified flashback panic. I'm researching bed bugs like the quirky experts on a CSI show. If I had multiple computer monitors inside a multi-million-dollar taxpayer funded glass and steel laboratory, I could complete the look. But it's just me and my Mac. I want to know everything about them. Will they come back? Are they zombies? How long can they go without feeding? I clearly want to avoid a repeat infestation, but now I'm on a mission to wipe them off the face of the Earth. I'm the Kyser Soze of bed begs. I don't simply want them dead... I want to kill their families, the bugs they associate with and anyone they had coffee with in the last decade. I want to burn their homes to the ground and lay waste to every piece of ground my boot steps on. I want to walk away from every place I roam, fiery explosions sailing into the sky as I calmly strut towards the camera... can of Raid bug spray in my hand... my face obscured in shadow.

Finally, I'm on my hands and knees with my eyeball face to face with the bed bug. I realized it was some kind of black seed that escaped from a piece of fruit—a kiwi or perhaps a rotten strawberry. Something that fell off the lip of my son, the seed tray of our bird, or most likely, my plate.

3

THE DOG DAYS OF SUMMER

We'd been in Texas so long that by the time Kevin and I got to the outskirts of El Paso, I'd assumed some sort of bastardized southern accent that I couldn't shake. Breaking down in Austin for 10 days, a friend took us in and his slow tone stuck. A New York minute on the Texan tongue can easily stretch to two. While at a gas station convenience store for fuel and snacks, I bid farewell to the clerk handing me change with a poorly drawn "Thank you kindly." His head cocked to the side like one might do while aiming a shotgun and asked, "Boy, where the hell are from?" I blinked, and in a deadpan response said "New York" and left without further discussion.

It was 1994. Kevin and I had just graduated from Syracuse University, so a never-ending road trip seemed like an appropriate reaction to such an event. Starting in the bowels of Onondoga County, New York, we'd driven down the east coast in Kevin's 1974 Oldsmobile 4-door Cutlass, a grey tank that floated like a fishing trawler. Having plowed over the corpse of a deer left in the middle of a dark country road in Georgia, we carried the stench of rotting venison with us through the remainder of our cross-country journey. With a bowler hat corked to my head, I took blurry photos with a Canon camera I'd failed to use properly, given to me by my father as a graduation gift. After Austin, we made the decision not to sleep till we got out of Texas, which sounds hilarious until three days go by and you're still in Texas. We made a pit stop at some godforsaken beige desert bathroom outpost and while washing my hands, noticed the next sink over was filled to the brim with insects. Overflowing. It was bizarre. Did they come up the drain? Was there a man walking about in a panic wondering where to dump his bucket of insects and chose the sink? I didn't know. It was shocking. Literally thousands of bugs... centipedes, roaches, beetles... everything... like a horror movie in an otherwise completely normal, clean rest room. I slowly backed out and sped away, haunted.

   After passing through El Paso, we headed up to White Sands, New Mexico, where it was so hot and the sand so bright, my lack of sleep induced hallucinations. We slept on the banks of the Rio Grande and in Truth or Consequences, New Mexico, drank a few beers with the forlorn locals and watched the Knicks lose to the Houston Rockets in game 7 of the NBA Championship. Then we zipped over to Arizona, a cool 119 degrees in the evenings. A few days later, we got a dingy motel in Vegas and hit the slots. In Caesar's Palace, the first crank I pulled hit $300. Didn't win a dime after that. I cobbled together a 3:00am dinner of scrambled eggs, shrimp cocktail and nachos and said to myself, "This isn't working anymore." We'd had just about enough of the road and Vegas is a town sure to wring the last vestige of road trip glamour from your previously plucky system. It was two months on the road and we were spent. We made a mad desert dash to Los Angeles, and in a matter of hours, we'd settled in at Kevin's house in Burbank, the end of the line.

The day after we arrived, Rachel, Kevin's girlfriend who we left in New Orleans, dropped a news bomb. Her father shocked his family by coming out of the closet. He declared that he'd never gotten over his one true love... his buddy from Viet Nam, who was killed in the line of duty. The entire week we visited, dad was holed up in a tiny TV room watching a Madonna tour video where her backup dancers consisted of 20 sweaty men, gyrating on stage... I was too stupid to see it then, but in hindsight... yea, I think he wore the tape to dust.

I snooped around Burbank, California, scoping the lay of the land—wondering how I could penetrate the studio walls—a nut trying to break into the asylum. I wanted to get into the movie biz somehow and staring at massive beige aircraft carrier buildings seemed like a good start. Like I'd be absorbed into the walls somehow. But after some careful assessment, scratching my head in front of what seemed like insurmountable walls of barbed-wire, I concluded it was probably best to head back to New York and reset. L.A. didn't vibe with me, which Kevin told me long before we got there. "You're too New York" he said... not sure if it was an insult or a compliment. To be "New York" is to have a certain character, or maybe idiosyncrasy... and I suppose I did. But I always felt worldly with the ability to fit anywhere. But he was right. L.A. is not for me. A square peg in a never-ending urban sprawl. The beaches were devoid of people, but the streets were packed with cars. I finally understood what Woody Allen was kvetching about in *Annie Hall*. Scanning a newspaper for one-way tickets to New York, an inconceivable thought in this day and age, I found one and walked to an office building and acquired it off some toothy lawyer for cash. Walking back, people looked at me horrified, mouths agape like I was washed in blood because it's true what they say... No ONE walks in L.A.

Returning to Long Island from L.A., I immediately hopped on my uncle's paint crew... a job that provided me with rent, beer and weed money all through college. Now that school was completed, with no books or art supplies to purchase, the money went directly to real-life items... rent, beer, weed and cocaine. Working with my uncle over the years, starting in high school, through college and into the working world, I worked with the same rotating cast of morality-shifting misfits. It's where I learned not only about hard physical labor, but about how our society works as a whole... our rich in relation to our poor, class systems and human nature in general. If you want to learn about life, get a physical labor job that requires you to enter people's homes. You'll discover a wide range of emotions... from pride to frustration, while being exposed to every kind of personality, from salt-of-the-Earth humility to confounding elitism. Nothing brings you up to speed like dealing with people's obsessive/compulsive disorders while standing in the middle of their living room, their entire life under plastic sheeting, assuring them "Everything is going to be alright." After a lifetime of schooling and mostly being sheltered, this was where I figured it all out.

Our fearless leader, my uncle Paul, was the living embodiment of Elwood Blues (Dan Ackroyd) from the movie *The Blues Brothers*. He wore sunglasses, drank endless cups of coffee and always had a cigarette glued to his lip. His van was essentially a mobile ashtray that happened to carry paint supplies. He was, and is, a brilliant guitarist who wanted to be in the music biz, but he took over a paint company and that's where he got snagged in the net of life... in the kaleidoscope of paint chips and cold aluminum ladders.

The first assignment that summer was a huge condominium complex in "the Pit" in Northport, New York. With their manicured lawns and giant glass atriums, the massive units bent around a finger inlet of water, surrounded by a horseshoe of large sloping dirt cliffs and trees that rose about 200 feet above sea level. All traffic on the main roads leading in could see the condos, and in turn, the condos could see any vehicle driving along the roads. My uncle's blue van could be spotted a mile before he got to the job site, providing ample time to dispose of beer cans and other evidence of tomfoolery. Our task was to cover a billion square feet of thirsty sea-side wood siding with Cabots dune grey semi-transparent stain with a paint gun that looked, and functioned like, a poorly designed robot from a terrible 1950s sci-fi film. It was a job so tedious and herculean, it felt like bailing water from the Titanic with a teacup.

To conquer the condos, we had to cut the job in two. Half one summer and half the following summer. A long con game. Other than my uncle and me, everyone came and went multiple times over the years... mostly because they were thrown off the job for drinking, drugs and at times, going completely AWOL on savage booze benders. On more than one occasion, Paul would wipe the slate clean in a tyrannical tirade and fire the entire crew in one fell swoop. Eventually they'd all come crawling back like street urchins, hats in hands, begging for more porridge. Because the condos were massive three-story, multi-unit megillahs, with work executed on baking roofs in the unforgiving sun, we needed fresh bodies to toss into the fire. The crew was mostly unemployable in other vocations, so they were always happy to return. Once you worked on the condos you knew how to handle them, so experience was king... no matter how drunk and stupid you were.

There is a myth that house painters are heavy drinkers. Some hypothesize that the smell of the paint and chemicals has something to do with it. Some say it's the mind-numbing labor that drives one to drink. I can't be sure *philosophically* why we drank, but we drank... *heavily*. If ever there was a book to be judged by its cover, it would be the common house painter. They wear a uniform speckled from head-to-toe in colored dots, which teeters in appearance from serious worker to circus clown. Painters provide a service in which they scour every inch of your house whether it be inside or out. They crawl on your roof, look in your windows, move your furniture and basically put you out. People have a fear of painters because unlike plumbers and refrigerator repairmen, they work in large groups. This makes the mischief level rise considerably. It can appear as if an entire crew of painters are happily swabbing your walls, when in actuality, one man has escaped and is rifling through the underwear drawer of every member of your family. They're into the husband's porn collection, tooling with the wife's vibrator and dipping into little Johnny's pot stash.

Painters are looked upon as slobs and vermin, but many blue-collar types like us were quite refined. In fact, we'd always start the mornings with conversations about film and literature. Who was reading what, and who had seen the new films... independent or blockbuster. I'm sure if you took a peek out your window and saw a semi-circle of scraggly looking riff-raff like us jawing over coffee, you'd be convinced we were planning in gory detail the best ways to rape and pillage the complex, when in actuality we were probably discussing if Martin Landau's performance in *Ed Wood* deserved the best supporting actor Oscar over Samuel L. Jackson in *Pulp Fiction*.

Purchased for a handful of pocket lint, our second work van was audaciously named The Eagle after the Apollo 11, even though it handled more like a drunken penguin. Essentially a crazy quilt on wheels, every panel on the jalopy was reclaimed from another van... some duct taped on, while others were rusting off. Kevin Roof, our mustached ex-navy foreman who had the dubious honor of driving it, picked us up every morning and bounced us to the job while we pinballed unanchored around the interior. The only seat other than the driver's was a swiveling deep-sea fishing chair mounted next to the sliding side door. Apparently, the previous owner was a nutty fisherman who'd pull up along any body of water and toss a line out. It was not unusual to be sitting in the fisherman's seat, spinning around at high speeds and have the side door fling open... the road and your life speeding before your very eyes. Because it was rusting away, the Eagle had random gaping holes in the floor. We'd mentally and physically prepare for work during morning commutes by preventing brushes and equipment from bouncing into the street. The Eagle, as one might surmise, did not receive warm welcomes from the condo people. Puttering through the iron gates and driving the long winding private road, we could see the look of every resident as they passed in their Jaguars and BMWs, their mouths open in astonishment. No matter how many times they saw the Eagle, it was like seeing it for the first time. She left a trail of oily black smoke so thick, it hovered like a storm cloud long after we'd passed. Combined with the collage of Grateful Dead stickers that adorned the windows, the thing screamed *arrest us*.

The condo complex formed a committee to oversee all things condo related. Everything from trash collection, lawn care maintenance, dog walker rotations and of course... watching over the painters. The committee consisted of retirees, silver-haired old biddies, rich housewives and what you can probably imagine as the stuffy, highfalutin old folks in the movie *Caddyshack*. So, there was plenty of free time to hawk over the painters and their activities. If there was a tenet complaint, they'd go to the committee, the committee would meet, then dispense justice accordingly. Free time + misplaced judicial aspirations = headaches. We upset just about every person in every condo unit, who'd blame us for things that would brain-cramp a quantum physicist. One couple accused us of causing their dishwasher to overflow while they were away on vacation, causing water damage to their photograph collection. We were two months away from reaching that unit. Apparently, we increased everyone's electricity and water bills by 500% while smashing their furniture to bits, mangling their prized flowers, killing their lawns and browning their bushes into tumbleweeds.

After riding a Wall Street trader all night, a prostitute ran onto the lawn and took a sitting mower for a topless joy ride. Our workmate Billy Campion ran down and joined her and the two whooped it up like a bachelor party. Needless to say, a *lot* of people watched the debauchery as it was 8:45 in the morning in full view of every breakfast table. Accused of bringing whores to the job site, we were almost thrown off the job. Now, I *know* blue color workers can be downright crude at times, but who is so depraved that they bring a prostitute to a job they're working on? Did they think we were substituting smoke breaks with sex breaks? Who can afford to pay a prostitute to join the crew and watch us paint all day while waiting to take care of our vulgar, lustful needs should they arise? Laborers can be stupid, but they know the value of a dollar better than anyone and giving sex workers money to watch you work is not a good return on your investment. But that was too much rational thinking for the committee and this is what can happen when there's a pack mentality. At times, the police were involved with some of the complaints. Detectives even! During our time there, we were falsely accused of...

- Stealing a home entertainment system (an independent interior painter moved it to a closet about 5 feet away from where it originally was)

- Stealing a bow and arrow set (any of us that wanted one already owned one)
- Stealing a set of ancient Chinese shadow puppets (Turns out a small child took them at a puppet show)
- Stealing food from someone's refrigerator (This was an outside paint job with no access to people's homes)
- Shitting in the bushes. (you don't shit where you work. There was a bathroom)

Here's something we were accused of that may or may not have been true...

- Sprayed a brand-new black BMW with Cabots dune grey stain (needed to pay for new paint job)
- Watched a personal trainer screw an old banker's hot young wife from a skylight while he was at work. (This one is true actually)

When the trainer came to the door and rang the bell of Unit 3, we were already sliding across the rooftop like Artful Dodgers. Weight distribution on a roof is crucial so as not to make it creak. It's also important to displace body weight around fragile structural areas such as skylights. Of greater importance still, is knowing the correlation of the sun between you and the floor of a condo below a skylight. All of this was known and executed to perfection. We clung to our choice spots ready to watch the action, but before we could get an eyeful, the distinctive shriek of car tires filled the air. Frozen, the starfish of painters surrounding the skylight couldn't move. Within seconds, the old man had bounded his car into the driveway and was at the door in the bat of an eye. We watched horrified as he blasted in and discovered the wife and trainer in their compromising positions. Never before have you seen a group of unathletic men scramble from a rooftop with such haste. I jumped two stories onto the ground and when I got there, the others were already there, painting the wall like they'd been there for hours. The front door slammed and the trainer jumped in his sports car and fled. The next day it got to the condo committee that the painters were drooling heavily on their skylights in hopes of fueling their masturbation material. We were embarrassed for sure but that was because we'd failed to assign a lookout, which is window-gazing 101.

  Multiple skylights peppered every roof and we were bound to see something... good or bad... like rooftop TVs. Except the programming was actual life. Your favorite program: the people down below. The skylights could give you amazing slices of life: kitchen disasters or living room furnishings gone wrong. Skylights above bathrooms were Russian Roulette. You dream of catching a glimpse of a gorgeous beauty stepping from the tub, but you're more likely to get a brain-seizing eyeful of someone resembling a poorly feathered chicken left in the rain. It is the fantasy of laborers far and wide to be seduced by a sexy homeowner on the job. The wife might want to have a romp while the husband's away... that sort of thing... it's the basis of the entire porn industry. Even the women fantasize about the UPS man, his thick thighs bursting through his summer shorts, delivering the packages exactly where she needs them. The wife and the trainer weren't the first time we'd seen affairs going on. Once in a great while, a painter will find themselves in the right place at the right time.

In 1992, a few summers prior to the condo job, we painted the interior of a humongous mansion for a doctor and his family. The obnoxious house had an elevator and with its creamy marble columns, grand rotating staircases and green walls, it resembled a massive $100 bill. One afternoon I found myself alone in the basement painting a closet in a maid's quarters. The house was usually streaming with plumbers and electricians, swarming about like worker ants. Like all big jobs, the end was in sight, and only a few minor touch-ups needed to be completed before calling it done. But I was alone... the only worker in the entire house that day.

The wife, a petite, blue-eyed blonde, barked my name from the top floor. I made my way from the far side of the house, up to the landing where she was waiting. Holding a metal rod, she asked me to step into the guest bedroom across from the master bedroom. She proceeded to rattle off what seemed to be a plethora of unrelated tidbits... she was running late, that her husband was in the city and the kids were at her mothers. She needed the rod and shower curtain installed in the guest shower and if I could do that for her, it would be great, because she had to take a shower before going to the airport to pick up some friends who were going to be using said guestroom.

As I began the installation process, she went to the master bedroom and undressed... with the door open. I looked over my shoulder to catch a glimpse of her nude body as she glided to the bathroom in a blur. This was not a mistake on her part. Water splashed on the new tile shower floor, which was evident as she also seemed to have accidentally left the bathroom door open. My mind started to race. Is this it? Does she want me to...? I could understand her desire. With my rippling 135-pound frame, jean shorts and oversized painter's cap facing backwards, I could lather any woman into a sexual frenzy. So, there I was in the guest bathroom, she's in her bathroom. Both doors are open. It was too much of a sign. My heart raced. She knew I was there and that I could easily see her. I tiptoed to the master bedroom door. I poked my eye around the edge, but the large glass shower was out of sight. I noticed her underwear laying openly on the floor, steam wafting over the garment like a seducing fog.

Then, I saw an entire scenario in my head... my uncle on the phone... the doctor screaming through the receiver on the other end. Paul holding the receiver away from his ear so as to not rupture an already damaged eardrum. We've been thrown off the job and would not be getting the last third of the payment for the back-breaking work. I would be the sole reason because I couldn't control my hungry, raw urge to dive into the shower and savagely fornicate with his wife. I'd be marked. Joked about at family dinners for decades to come. Forced into Hari-kiri, having brought shame to the family name. With clarity, I picked up my paint bucket, which I'd left in the hallway, and made my way to the middle of the lobby. When the water stopped, I hollered from the bottom of the stairs.

"Need anything else?"

Perhaps cunnilingus, or horizontal mambo lessons?

She shouted "No," and slammed the bedroom door as hard as she could. Most definitely in anger. I slinked back to the maid's quarters where I folded myself inside a closet and finished the interior. Next day, I told the crew what happened, but none of them believed me in the slightest... even after carefully displaying all the evidence. All in my imagination, they told me. Ultimately, I made the right choice. It could have easily been a setup to get us thrown off the job and not pay the final lump sum for the work. I wouldn't put it past anyone. But the thought of living out a dream that only happens in bad pornographic movies would have been a delight. But I missed my opportunity and I wouldn't get another one because I never planned to deliver pizzas.

•••

One of the many great duties of the painter besides the obvious scraping, painting and filing of police reports, is who is going to get lunch. We weren't a brown bag kind of crew. No one thought more than four or five hours ahead, so planning lunch a full day in advance was ludicrous. The lunch run assignment had its pros and cons. You would usually get lunch orders where sandwiches had no fewer than six or seven ingredients. And that was for five or six chubby guys. And that's if we got *sandwiches*. Meals like meatloaf and mashed potatoes with vegetables were a common order... with a chocolate chip cookie and a pint of milk for desert... washed down with a 64-ounce bottle of Gatorade. We'd stuff ourselves and curse America for never adopting the siesta into its culture.

But the lunch run also gave you the freedom to venture out where breathing, thriving people gathered. Townsfolk, whistling joyfully as they went about their day. The sound of children laughing and a dog playfully barking as it fetched a

Frisbee. These were the things you saw and heard when you removed a respirator and goggles and got into a motor vehicle. The deli was always a hub of action. You'd always meet a girl who was getting her cooler filled with Italian heroes and beer; preparing to jump into a sleek water vessel piloted by her boyfriend. We always had more in common with the deli counter girls. They too were grinding away for money... saving to move on or up in the world, or to simply get the hell out of there. I often got the call to make the lunch run because I rarely screwed up the orders. I had this trick where I would write the order down on paper. Without the aid of stenography, a lunch order could run a few pages deep. It's not pretty to see a sweaty, grown man whine because he didn't get his cookie. Jerry was usually the most vehement about having an order screwed up. He was very specific about what he wanted and how it should be prepared. Yet, when Jerry was the one who made a lunch run, he'd completely disregard your order and get whatever he wanted. You ordered roast beef and Swiss on rye? You got ham. You ordered a Seven Up? You got Coke. Everyone would end up getting the same thing because he didn't bother to write down anyone's order and instead, ordered five 'bologna specials.' Then he'd pocket the change and tell you all he had was a twenty-dollar bill and couldn't break it. This was after he'd been missing for an hour making "phone calls" which is code for 'drinking at the bar.' This is why I always went for lunch.

    You can always tell when the summer is coming to an end. You don't have to look at a calendar or calculate the wind. The surest way to know is when there is a sudden lack of people around. The college kids go back to school, boats get moored and the dogs wistfully place their Frisbees into the storage bin. Within a week, all the cute girls you saw at the deli and buzzing around town at night in their tiny short shorts are mysteriously gone. The beach is devoid of fresh lean bodies, yet brimming with leather bag looking old folks. The bars and clubs at night are stocked with only a few middle-aged drunks peppered throughout. They were always there of course... they were just being obscured by hot, young twenty-year-olds. But then there's an eerie, empty feeling because the boys of summer are all gone and you're still around. Like you've been left behind. Abandoned. And your summer job becomes an actual job. The tinge of autumn hits your skin and your mortality creeps up on you like a light denim jacket. The months painting turned into years and evaporated into thin air like turpentine fumes. Time flies when you're having fun, drinking like a fish and snorting piles of cocaine. The winters split the time and indoor jobs were akin to hibernation till we could be released outdoors again. Painting provided steady work and good money till I could save enough to go somewhere besides where I was.

To battle the cold Fall and Winter nights, I shacked up with Crystal, a bona fide mad woman. Crystal was a gorgeous Korean who was adopted and raised by Sicilians. She had a shrill, Long Island Italian accent and was outrageously temperamental. She was also a booze-guzzling, pill popping, coke snorting, crack smoking, chronically lying, bulimic man-magnet. Somehow, she took a liking to me. I was never sure why we were together. She'd built a castle of lies that would crumble every time she spoke. Stories of incest, rape, marriage, miscarriage, kidnapping, childbirth, jail, drug abuse and rehab swirled endlessly and could never be traced to any basis in fact. She repeatedly switched boyfriends... bouncing between myself and others at the drop of a hat. One night in a dramatic plea, she begged me to take her away where no one knew us.

"Please, let's just get out of here, I can't stand this town!" she wailed, slamming endless amounts of pill bottles and sunglass cases into her bottomless purse.

We got on the road and drove until we finally stopped at some seedy dive bar in a no-name stretch of town. While shooting pool, a man slapped his hand in the middle of the table.

"Crystal, why don't you return my calls?"

It was impossible to go somewhere she wasn't known.

Hanging out with Crystal was compounding my already reckless behavior. We loved to drink and do drugs and she had a plethora of drugs at her disposal. Besides doing massive amounts of coke and crack, she also took Valium, Xanax and Percocet, drank it all down with vodka and topped it off with a spritz of her steroid asthma inhaler. She also smoked two packs of Marlboro Reds a day. She was an absolute train wreck and I was along for the ride... popping pills and smoking crack right along with her in the caboose. I'm not sure either of us had anything in common other than our appetite for drugs and our physical attraction. I honestly can't remember anything we said to each other the entire time we hung out. I pretty much just tried to get her into bed all the time, but rarely did because we were both too inebriated to do anything.

For my birthday, her surprise gift for me was a threesome with her friend Heather. The gift that keeps on giving... in stories to your friends and hopefully not a sexually transmitted disease. Heather was a lovely piece of blonde trailer trash who often rode precariously between the line of model gorgeous and down-and-out cracked mirror skank. At our drinking hole, Vanderbilts, they fussed over me... took turns kissing and hugging me.

Heather said, "I'm not wearing any underwear."

She guided my hand between her legs to see she wasn't lying. Crystal grabbed my collar and dragged me to the ladies' room to do coke. After more drinks we left. Crystal's parents were out of town. After more coke and booze, we were in the basement on a large guest bed. The girls excused themselves and returned wearing sexy lingerie. We attacked each other... squirming naked on the bed. I was giving my attention to both when I made a painful discovery... I couldn't get it up! I'd snorted too much cocaine. There I was naked on a king-sized bed with two gorgeous girls and I was unable to get my soldier to stand at attention... the wish of every heterosexual male on the entire planet up in smoke... or up my nose. The great American tragedy.

A week later Heather was found dead in a motel. She was speed balling with strangers and overdosed. The police found her alone and abandoned to die by herself. Crystal was destroyed.

•••

Soon after, Crystal and I eventually drifted apart. It

was all too much. After all the debauchery, I really started focusing on a future... which meant halving my drinking and doubling my portfolio. Besides painting and the occasional stint as a photographer's assistant, I filled the coffers bartending the bleak Wednesday night shift at Vanderbilts. Bartending is another vocation you can fall on when your regularly scheduled life gets interrupted. I was advised to "never burn your paint clothes and always keep a cocktail guide on your shelf." Truer words were never spoken.

One particularly slow shift as the clock rounded midnight, the door swung open and a hulking mass lumbered in. He looked rough... body as thick as a tree trunk, with arms like thighs. His curly reddish-brown hair was pressed and matted around his giant skull like he'd been wetted and dried multiple times. The knotted rusty hair spread down across his wide, muscular face into a beard. His wild eyebrows were tattered above his dark eye sockets. His eyes glowing like two piss holes in the snow. He sat at the bar, even spacing between the only two people in the place, Greg and Wally... two regulars. His dirty hand shot out to Wally, who obliged and shook it. I could tell from the sound of Wally's voice that he wasn't expecting to see this man ever again.

"I just got out of jail," the mass growled, opening his flannel jacket superman-style... revealing an orange jumpsuit.

Normally when you're released from a respectable prison system, they return your street clothes. This revelation seemed like a daunting development. Was he released or did he escape? We weren't about to ask.

He shot me a look and my spine froze. If vibes were

measured on a Richter scale, we'd be somewhere amid San Francisco 1906 and the end of the world. He demanded beer and tequila. I placed them down and asked him for 6 bucks. His face clenched like a fist. This was not the response he wanted. He was stinking drunk already and wasn't expecting to pay.

"I've got this one" Wally interrupted and slid his $10 on the bar towards me.

The mass looked me over uninvitingly... ran his hand over his face from eyebrows to chin and asked my name.

"A.J." I squeaked.

"What?" he barked, like I'd spoken Chinese.

"A.J." Wally said with a rescue, "He's alright."

The mass wasn't impressed. I poured him another shot and let any compensation pass by. His fist hammered the bar as he turned to Greg to his right.

"So, what the hell is going on around here?" It was a rhetorical question.

After some tense light banter, the convict threw a rumbled $20 on the bar as a tip to drink for free all night. I took the money and put it in my metal tip bucket. It wasn't a problem. How much could he drink? Four beers and a couple of shots? Five beers and three shots? Any amount seemed enough to let him leave without a problem. To this day I'm not sure how much he actually drank, but it must have been more then I could have imagined, because I decided to speak up. I told him I couldn't serve him free anymore. You can imagine how that news went down. It didn't. I poked the sleeping bear. His mouth bent to a scowl... his eyes squinted into slits. Wally looked at me hopelessly. Greg's eyes turned to observe the ceiling. The convict thrust his chest to the bar and launched his hand out.

"Give me that fuckin' twenty back, you pussy!"

I turned calmly, fished the $20 from my metal tip can and placed the wrinkled bill and on the bar.

"I gave you this as a tip, why you disrespect me like that, huh?" he asked in a broken-hearted plea.

"I appreciate the tip" I said calmly, "but you're gonna drink two hundred dollars' worth of alcohol. I'll lose my job."

This rational was a spike in the heart of his reasoning. His blood boiled. My pulse pumped in my neck. He cocked back... his chest blowing out like a toad... his eyes full of hate. He stood and lifted his jacket to reveal the grip of a revolver tucked deep in the waistband of his dirty jeans. I was frozen... suffering a paralyzing out of body experience. Wally was shocked... his hands up like a mime trapped in a box. Greg seemed strangely at ease, perhaps the only way to approach the situation.

"I don't think you should have that in here" Greg stated, matter-of-factly. "You could get in serious trouble."

The convict's eyes shifted back and forth... then to me... Greg's words ringing in his head. The convict realized he took it too far. It's just a drink and I was just a bartender, but I knew men have killed and gone to prison for lesser reasons. Just as calmly as he'd yanked his jacket up, he pulled it back down, his expression unchanged. He swigged the last of his beer and headed to the door. As he got to there, he looked back and pointed at the three of us.

"If you say shit to anyone about this, I'll fuckin' kill you." Then he was gone.

The three of us bolted to the door. Greg got there first and locked it... placed his head against the window to angle his view down the street.

"He's gooone!" He declared, like a night watchman calling out the hour.

A call to the police was made, but a patrolman never came by. Greg and Wally stayed with me till closing. Every new customer who tried to enter was met with a locked door till they were allowed entry. I drank all night and woke a few days later, hungover and drained.

I drifted to my uncle Paul's house a few streets over and knocked on the back door. He was in the kitchen fussing over a freshly baked cheesecake.

"You wanna a cup of my special kaw-fee?" he offered.

It should be noted that when anyone offers you a cup of their "special coffee," it simply means that instead of the recommended two or three scoops, they dump in eight or nine scoops. He poured me a cup darker than a black hole. I poured a shot of cream, which did nothing to change the color, and ate a creamy slice of cheesecake for breakfast. He makes good cheesecake.

I'd worked with Paul on and off for eight years. I learned a lot from being on the job with my uncle. I learned about painting to be sure... a skill that is useful all through life. But I learned about business, people, success, failure, tolerance and determination. It was a good job to start my working life with. Physical labor is the job of real people. Jesus was a simple carpenter. I'm sure you've heard that before. Who in your life hasn't made the analogy about Jesus being a carpenter? Even if just in jest: "I just built this bookshelf." "Hey, Jesus was a carpenter." Well, I like to look at Michelangelo as a house painter. He did the inside of the Sistine Chapel. Sure, his work was a little more complex than just rolling latex white, but he did the whole thing himself.

After all the work and drugs and sheer lunacy, it was time to move on. I told Paul I was getting a job in Manhattan. He was supportive, as always. You know things are bad when you move *to* New York City to escape drugs and gun violence.

BUGGIN' OUT

4

RAH-RAH, SIS BOOM BAH!

Ever have someone tell you where they went to college and not only have you never heard of it, you have no idea where it could possibly be in the world or if it even exists? Almost like a test to see if you're a liar.

"Where'd you go to school?" you ask innocently.

"Sprenson" they say proudly and nodding confidently.

The information is presented like one might announce a dish's secret ingredient. "Cardamom."

You nod back, raise your eyebrows... release a confident "ohhh" with a hint of pleasant surprise. Assure them it was an excellent choice for a 17-year-old to make. Then you bullshit and say "good school" even though you have no idea what the university's curriculum could possibly be. You may try to project what the school's specialty might be based on the profession of the person divulging the information.

"Yes, Sprenson is well-known for... accounting?"

"I went for tree surgery but ended up in accounting after an internship."

My friend Jessica, who I worked with at a marketing firm, went to school for marine biology but morphed into the world advertising and design, so it's not out of left field. Sometimes you may try and guess where the school is located based on the name.

"Sprenson, that's in North Dako..."

"Texas"

"Right, northern Texa..."

"It's in southern Texas."

"Exactly, the northern part of... southern Texas."

Acknowledging the school regardless of its familiarity to you is just good manners. Surely, they've put themselves and their family in years of crippling debt to educate themselves. They deserve to have you lie and give your completely worthless stamp of approval. You have to say, "good school" and nod.

What are you supposed to say when someone tells you they went to Syracuse University?

"Syracuse! What the hell did you go there for? Jesus, why didn't you pool your money in a pile and light it on fire? Did they give you a free bowl of soup with your degree? Well, good luck out there... it's a cruel and remorseless world."

No, of course not. You nod and say "I thought about going there myself but decided to go to Harvard instead" -- like the polite person you are. Besides, you didn't want to go to school in Pennsylvania and decided the Boston area had a better climate for you.

At a party a woman told me where she schooled with

such confidence, she told me the information looking at me over her thick-rimmed glasses. When I admitted my unfamiliarity with that cultural institute of higher learning, her faced crushed like a paper bag. I decided not to lie, and she frowned in disappointment at my woeful lack of university knowledge. She said enrollment was only about 800 students, which confused me further. Was she saying it was so prestigious that only the smartest of the smart are admitted and this is common knowledge to everyone -- or was it supporting my case by showing how insignificant it was among the 99,000 colleges and universities across the United States? I'll never know. People *love* to tell you about their school because they want to brag about how smart they are or how much better of a sports program they have compared to the half-rate school you attended. Like they're the dean of admissions or the athletic director.

"We made it to the '*I Can't Believe It's Not Butter*' Bowl with our second string quarterback."

Is that right, coach?

During the course of a conversation, someone will toss their school in the mix because it relates to the topic somehow. "Duke University? I went to Bedlam Dobbins!" Again, there's nodding and "ohhhs." Because Bedlam Dobbins is... in North Carolina? Has a Blue Devil as a mascot? Has a notorious hazing death hanging over it like a dark cloud?

Sometimes people will just shout a state they went to college.

"I went to Florida!" Like that narrows it down. Florida State? Florida University? University of Florida? They'll tell you with a dismissive chuckle, "There's only one Florida." Which means you'll never know because you won't ask.

Once the Super Bowl ends, there's a distinctive slumber in the sports world, which electrifies in spring by what is called March Madness. I'm sure you've heard of it. That's when college basketball reaches its nadir and a complex tier bracket appears with the names of all the colleges entering the elimination tournament. If you've had trouble identifying colleges and their locations before, crack a Milwaukee's Best Light and scroll through the championship bracket. It's guaranteed to leave your brain knotted.

"Baylor! That's in Oregon... or maybe... Oklahoma?"

Many schools have their name in it, like Tennessee. But some are general areas, like Northwestern.

"Northwestern... that's in... Seattle? Utah? Where is Utah? Where's my map?"

Terrible geography aside, unless you're intimately involved with college sports, some of these schools are a mystery. Especially when you start hitting the acronyms. VCU vs. ODU! LSU vs. DBU! That's when faking knowledge of a school can get dicey.

"I went to UCSB!" University of Christian Submarine Battalions? That's a good school!

Go to any NCAA Men's Basketball bracket from the past decade and I can assure you there's a school or five that will stump you. McNeese? Presbyterian? Wofford? Butler? Murray State? I'm no cartographer, but I'm pretty sure none of our 50 states is even called Murray.

If you find yourself stumped by some of these schools, let me tell you about Division II and Division III sports. That's where the line of reality blurs. If you've ever watched a film about sports, you'll invariably see one about baseball or football in which getting the rights to real American sports teams was either too expensive or simply not possible. So, they create one for the film. Sometimes they're nameless teams with a number on their cap. Another film may have a creative department and they design their own mascot and logo. But it seems off.

My Brazilian wife, who is as ignorant of American sports as anyone, has at least heard of the New York Yankees and the Pittsburgh Steelers. But when she sees a team in a film called the Stompers, she knows something's off. Even people without televisions have seen the large green Muppet-like Philly Fanatic tumbling around the Philadelphia Phillies stadium. But create a mascot of a turkey or a googly-eyed catcher's mitt, and the suspension of disbelief crumbles. That's Division II and III sports in a nutshell. Something just seems off.

For some unknown reason, Division II and III are not allowed to have decent names and mascots for their programs. It's not written down, like on paper or anything; it just seems to be the way. Nor are they allowed to have good TV time slots. Awaken before the sun and flip on the television, you may catch the last half of the Wisconsin Rusty Nails vs the Colorado Magenta Frogs.

Eating breakfast one weekend at the counter of a local greasy spoon, my son and I caught a football game versus two nameless animal teams played on a fluorescent lime-green field. Mixed with charred corned beef hash and coffee, the effect was downright hallucinatory. My son asked what animals they were, based on the logos, and my answers varied from canary heads to hurdling possums. As the camera panned across the near-empty stadium, a Viking posed for the audience with a rage and intensity that did not match the level of game play on the field. Why a Viking? Was more than one game being played in the stadium that day? Was he early? Is he an actual Viking? Later, another camera pan revealed our Viking hero texting on his phone, which broke the illusion completely. Someone tapped his shoulder to announce his reappearance on the jumbotron, but the Schwarznegger-esque flexing of his trapezius muscles was unconvincing. The thrill was gone.

    I assume when it comes to choosing mascots and names, there's an enormous process. Mainly because there's gazillions of dollars at stake. There's committees and voting and then there's some sort of submission and approval process. Suited people around large conference tables making important decisions. Probably chewing giant cigars with access to ejector seat buttons.

    "We need to name our athletes the Bison or Lightning Bolts! Huh? Something aggressive and powerful" they'd shout, pounding coffee cups off the table.

    "I don't know, the Tenderloins has a nice ring to it."

    You'd think schools would try and have gladiatorial battles on the field against the Titans or the Broncos. Yet when I turn on the TV I see an immovable object like a tree doing battle on the gridiron against an entity like the wind or a sunray. Or a pickle is locking horns with a cobbler or an early American settler that's been dead for 400 years. Some of this is local history but some of it is the unfortunate decision to bring the public into the naming process. "Name our school mascot!" Get a poor ballot showing and your local high school team is now the Dolphins even though you live in the flatlands where wheat grows in endless waves of grain. It's possible that a clique of popular 11 year-old girls could be responsible for the high school branding that lingers for generations.

Joe Biden and I both graduated from Syracuse University. Comparisons end there. Back in Joe's day, Syracuse's mascot was the Native American *Saltine Warrior*, dismissed in the early days of racist awareness. Then they became the Syracuse Orangemen and their mascot was an Orangeman... a large orange ball with legs and a snappy blue ball cap. To modernize and incorporate inclusion, the university eliminated the 'men/man' from their name and became simply the Syracuse Orange. Before, the Syracuse Orangeman just seemed like orange the color, but now that he's the Syracuse Orange, he seems more like the fruit. I say 'him' because his name is Otto. Unfortunately, you couldn't grow an orange in Syracuse if you had a line-up of the world's most brilliant botanists working around the clock. Syracuse starts dropping snow on October first and it doesn't stop its unrelenting glaze until May first. I'm not a farmer, but I don't think oranges thrive in that kind of environment. The school can't uproot and move to Florida where oranges grow through your living room window, and Syracuse University can't change course and be a different entity... everything in Syracuse is orange! So, we'll just put our heads down and soldier on, proudly displaying our orange and blue and waving to Otto, the chipper Syracuse Orange who continues to inspire hope from the sidelines with his giant smile and dazzling googly eyes.

Early in my marriage, I was sitting on my couch watching some basketball and chomping on a bag of Funyuns when my wife entered and started yelling at me. I couldn't decipher everything that she was saying because I was busy watching the game on full volume, but the gist of her beef was that she couldn't fathom that it was June and that I was still watching college basketball. I assured her that college basketball was long over and this was NBA basketball. *Professional* basketball.

This did not appease her one iota.

It led to questions. Lots of questions.

"When is this season going to end?" she cried.

"In about three weeks." I told her, gently patting her hand. She nearly hit the roof on that bit of news. Then when I told her that I'd start watching baseball after basketball season ended, she nearly crumbled to the floor in a heap. Then, when I informed her that when the baseball season ended, the football season really started to heat up, she went to the computer and began shopping for plane tickets to the Bahamas. And she let it be known that it was a ticket for one.

I can't blame her. The sports seasons bleed into one another and if you're a sports fan, this is heaven, and if not, it's a constant cheering background din. Sports are on TV basically all the time, but so are bad reality shows that I have to suffer through, like *The Real Plastic Bitches of Beverly Hills* or *The Kardashians Do Dallas*.

Every time my wife has the remote, she's watching shows about a pack of frisky little people or how to remodel a house with dried mud and stuff laying around the dig sight. We don't always argue about the television programming because we have shows we watch together. But I realize there has to be a compromise. She knows I'm a sports nut, but I have to pick and choose the best sports to watch or I'd be in front of the TV all day and night.

To ease her worried mind, I explained my sports programming hierarchy.

I told her straight up that outside of a few college basketball games during March Madness, I didn't watch college sports *at all*. Right then and there, I eliminated 50% of the sports world. She could have thanked me then, but I needed to convince her further. Next was to tell her that I'm not a huge baseball fan and that I don't really watch that much of it. Baseball has 162 regular season games. If my team was good enough to make the playoffs, play every game of the playoffs, and even win the World Series, my team would play 183 games total.

"183 games?!" she cried. "Yeah," I said sheepishly, finally hearing myself.

Her jaw nearly hit the floor. She could not fathom the amount of games played in baseball.

But that's why I started with baseball; it's the benchmark to get the negotiations going. Before she attained total disbelief, I said I enjoyed basketball, and that the NBA had far less games than baseball. As a Knicks fan, if my team played the whole season, made the playoffs and played in every possible playoff game, they'd *only* play 110 games. She was upset, but compared to baseball, this was a huge difference. While these numbers were still fresh in her mind, I told her my favorite sport was NFL Football and they play just a measly 16 games a season. When she heard that news, she almost shed a tear of joy. NFL Football was only on once a week, on Sundays, and that the rest of the week was free and clear... except Monday nights... and occasionally Thursday nights... and then later on in the season, Saturdays. But if my team played all season and then every game of the playoffs plus the Super Bowl, it's a paltry 20 games! She was overjoyed at this news! I also informed her that my favorite team was the awful New York Jets who rarely made the playoffs, so she really had nothing to worry about. We'd be free to go skiing or participate in other winter activities right after the Christmas season.

Continuing the list: Hockey only required my attention for five games of the Stanley Cup Finals. I only watched the four major tournaments in golf, and the US Open Tennis finals for each sex and that was only two events! I concluded with The World Cup, which was on once every *four years*... When she heard that she nearly leapt into my arms with glee. These are the types of guidelines you need to layout for your significant other if they're overwhelmed by the amount of sports you watch.

My wife being from Brazil, they have one sport. Football. Or as we call it in America, soccer. Having lived in New York for 16 years, it was my weekly duty to educate a foreigner as to why Americans call a sport that seems to be completely played with one's hands football, and why we didn't call a sport played completely with one's foot football. The answers never satisfied. I was given suggestions of calling it handball, but I think it's too late. I don't have any power in these decisions and I'm not on the voting committee. But Brazil is a football powerhouse and I'm a dedicated fan by marriage. If Brazil is deep into the World Cup, I'm shouting at the TV like I was raised on a steady diet of rice and beans in a small village outside Sao Paulo.

We watch sports like football and basketball because it's our inherent nature to make war and sports quench those desires by satiating our bloodlust vicariously. Sounds dramatic, but it's true. Sports prevent us from killing each other when someone else cuts in front of us in traffic. We get out that everyday rage by watching other men knock the living shit out of one another on a field. It's how we get out our frustrations with life. We live our lives in constant competition and we don't even know it—which grocery store line is moving faster? Can I beat this yellow light? And can I run across the street before the red hand symbol on the cross walk stops blinking?

One thing that makes sports so enjoyable to many, if they be leisure or hardcore sports, professional or college level, is our ability to know that there will be a champion in the end -- a final level that will culminate in a trophy, with celebrating and confetti. I find myself riveted to competition events on television that blind me to everything happening around me. Things like the World Beard and Moustache Championship. That's the one where men pomade their facial hair into contorted abstract geometric squiggles. As competitive humans, we enjoy competition on many different levels. Many of these, "Leisure Sports" like pool, darts and cards, don't always translate to television viewing. For many, watching poker, bowling or golf is like watching a steak marinate. Which may be around the corner in future Food Network competitions. Why they're televised at all is a mystery to many, but with 24 hours in a day and 15,000 channels to choose from, it's not difficult to understand why everything under the sun is on the TV. I suppose someone wants to watch the National Checkers Championship League or know who are the United Dominoes Competition Finalists. These activities don't always capture the attention of the masses, but football does. It's fast, hard-hitting and has excitement. Chess, not so much.

But I don't know. Maybe for some, watching the Green Bay Packers battle it out with the Chicago Bears is just as exhilarating and brutal as watching two women on the Food Network bake a dessert for a $10,000 prize. The sport of football and cooking have many similarities. A lot of blood, sweat and tears are left on the floor, emotions run high and everyone is exhausted. But most importantly, there's a winner and a loser, and that's just how we like it. In the end, our bracket tiers are filled in, teams have been eliminated, and standing triumphant on the highest pedestal... is the champion.

5

30 YEARS AND COUNTING...

When Tanya Woldbeck, our bubbly blond go-to cheerleader and organizer started the 30-year reunion push for Huntington High's class of 1989, I was reluctant to get emotionally involved. Understandable to many people for many reasons, I'm sure. Besides the constant feeling that I'm not a fully-formed person yet at the tender age of 47, I was absolutely convinced I couldn't match peoples' names to their faces.

I'm older for sure... not senile, but my memory is going. If one fresh bit of data enters my cranium, one older piece of info gets booted out. There's only so much space in the old noodle. The info that gets erased is usually valuable... like a distant cousin's name. The script for the 1984 movie *The Last Starfighter*? Seared right onto the cerebellum like a branding iron.

The frequent Facebook posts about who was coming to the reunion became a sick joke to me. "Sara So-and-So is coming!" Who? Was that a real person? "William Hgsdbkjhwbdck got his ticket!" I went to high school with that person? Pulling out my yearbook, I scanned these names. Some weren't even in there. Did they miss photo day? Who misses photo day? Was there a makeup photo day? Even the names I did recognize I couldn't recall the face -- and as an artist, I'm pretty good with faces. At least I think I am. My yearbook could be a showcase of Civil War tintypes. A tome of ancient humans. The children of a forgotten era. I did the 10-year reunion, which was a stones' throw away from graduation itself. The 20th was a party where we literally out-drank the restaurant's bar inventory, forcing them to buy more beer and alcohol. And when we drank all that, they simply turned the lights off. That place is now out of business. I'm not sure it's related.

These reunions can be a lot of "Hi! How are?!" then walking away thinking, "I don't care." I didn't care and I still don't. I have affection for a few. Old friends. I still see some of them once in a while. But Sara So-and-So? I can't talk to her! What the hell are we going to talk about? Bed bugs? How precious time is and how I'm wasting it talking with her? No, thank you. I only schooled with these people. They're not my family. How do they affect me? Are they good people? Do they recycle? Have they killed anyone?

When you're unclear of your identity, with no vision about your future, or what you might actually be becoming as a human being, then a high school reunion seems like a terrible idea. Shouldn't we all be rock-solid and completely conscious of who we are by this point? I mean, how do you properly answer the tough questions when your mind is swirling with uncertainty? Tough questions like "How are you?" No one wants to hear your problems. Not financial, not personal, and certainly not a detailed analysis of your crumbling ego. It doesn't fly in polite company. So, you grin, lie and nod... *over-nod* if you have to and say, "Great" enthusiastically to convince them completely. Then locate the bartender.

•••

My wife made it abundantly clear that she'd prefer to learn the art of sword swallowing than go to this reunion with me. If I could hardly muster the inspiration to go myself, why would she? It's a blessing in disguise as it frees me from endlessly introducing her to near strangers over thumping 80s beats. Because I'd not fully committed to the reunion till the last minute, the event didn't weigh me down with handwringing 'what-if' thoughts or imagined disastrous scenarios. I simply walked into it calmly without any preconceived notions. Like splaying back into a confident workshop trust fall, or a walk down Death Row.

The weekend blows through like a fever dream. It magically appears on Friday evening. I rush home from work, toss back spaghetti, kiss my family goodbye and hop in the car. Festivities start by painting 'The Rock,' a large boulder planted at the entrance (or is it the exit) of our high school where every two to four weeks a squadron ninjas along and paints town-legalized graffiti messages. They range from reunion info to wishes of good luck... and display which graduates can afford to go to what universities while others rot at local dead-end jobs.

Having arranged the meeting beforehand, Tanya texts "What's your ETA?" and I reply "Now!" as I zip around the corner... my balding, underinflated tires howling as I screech my four-cylinder engine to a stop with a cough. One hopes to return to a reunion driving their vintage cherry red '65 Ford Mustang convertible, or a brand-new Mercedes Benz SL in British Racing Green. Not me. Green, yes... metallic green. But that's coated around my 2010 Honda CRV. The hood is splattered with sap from a gnarly 300-year-old pine tree that jizzed all over it like a porn star. That horror movie tree, which I was forced to park under for years, would occasionally drop a sticky 14 ounce pine cone grenade that left a smattering of dents and dings on the hood as well, slowly decreasing the car's value with every bonk.

I hop out to a cluster of people waiting for me, the artist, to start the paint job. Tanya and the others have coated the rock in glowing white paint... a blank canvas ready to be blessed. I shake a few hands and call people, *man* and *whatsup* to avoid the inevitable embarrassment of calling Eric > Fred and Susan > Margaret. I'm terrible with names. Atrocious. I can't remember more than two names at the same time.

Everyone is terrible with names. So why are we all so embarrassed about it? Have you ever been introduced to a group of eight or nine people and stopped absorbing their names after shaking hands with person *number two* because you know, you're never going to remember their names?

I tell myself that I know all these people, but I just haven't thought about them in three decades... and their faces are different. But the same. It's horribly confusing. You say to yourself "didn't we go to high school together?" and the answer is obviously yes. But you're more concerned with smiling, nodding and being polite... giving a proper handshake. Firm and in control. Not too hard, not too soft. Firm. Good smile. Solid eye contact... not a deep stare! Say "hey" and disengage quickly, knowing there's someone next to them waiting for a handshake. They're in your peripheral vision. Waiting. Smiling too! Hand is out. You can't do all that *and* absorb people's names. That's like rubbing your stomach and patting your head... while doing your taxes.

Some faces I remember. Some I don't. Right from the jump, Alice Schulver reminds me that our cousins used to be married. I panic and say, 'My cousin Christen!" She looks at me disappointed and says "No." I believe she lowered her eyes and shook her head... like my mother did when she first saw my pierced ear. "Your cousin Mark was married to my cousin Janice," she re-informs me. It all floods back. Stupid! Yes. Of course! Janice. Of course I remember Janice. I used to do cocaine with her after the divorce. Maybe that's why I forgot... cocaine brain damage. I didn't tell Alice about the cocaine part. But I told her Mark died. Wasn't a great conversation, to be honest. But my fears are immediately realized. I can't even remember a connection as strong as my cousin Mark being married to Alice's cousin Janice. This is an ominous sign.

But I recover and scramble to the paint cans and sketch the school's Blue Devil mascot wearing 80s-styled shutter glasses and scrolling a zippy *RAD* above his head. Everyone snatches a can of spray paint and scribbles squiggle shapes and tags their name. I finish it off with highlights of neon orange. It ends up a few days later in the Long Island rag, *Newsday*. I couldn't be more proud.

Carl invites us to his parent's house, so we funnel over to their beautiful Victorian home in Huntington Bay. His parents are gracious and progressive. We drink, smoke some weed, nibble on crackers and catch up. His father tells me how whiskey is made then shows me his insanely rare Alfa Romeo, which is worth more than my internal organs if you lined them up in a row in freezer.

People filter in. Friends from the past... familiar faces. Vance, Alice again, Rebecca, Julie and some others. A pre-reunion reunion. Like hors d'oeuvre. A sampling. Easier to divide and conquer. Carl's neighbor, a guy a year ahead of us at school, remembers me, but I don't remember him. His face seems to be a permanent scowl. He's genuinely upset I don't remember him. Insulted even. "You really don't remember me?" he repeats indignantly across the cheese platter. I don't and I apologize, but I'm not sure why. Perhaps to mend his wounded ego. If I can't recognize my father's cousin at a family reunion, why would I remember Carl's neighbor? Carl's father wisely bails me from the quibble by educating me on tequila processing. This man knows me so well. We refresh our drinks at the makeshift folding table bar, a concoction of whiskey and tequila, and continue to mingle.

I left just before 10 O'clock... conscious to keep my liver in tip-top shape. It undoubtedly looks like the lung of an 80-year-old filterless smoker. Something you'd see in a classroom propaganda film to prevent kids from drinking. I know very well I need my immune system in high-functioning order. I'll need the brave shield of alcohol to protect me from the battle of the kind rewind. The rock painting and cocktail party was a gentle icebreaker. I'd already constructed some believable stories as to why I couldn't remember people's names... a devastating blow to the head with a side of frozen beef... a bad batch of mercury-laced crack which disabled 25% of my rear lobe. I decide not to use them. I decide right then and there that I'm not going to fake it with names. I'm just going to tell people I don't recall their names and if necessary, tell them flat-out I don't remember them *at all*. I don't give a shit. We're adults. Well, they're adults. I'm 12, but I play an adult in real life!

•••

Saturday Night... The Reunion. Sounds like the opening of a bad slasher film. I begin at the bar Mehann's, a spacious Irish pub with a giant horseshoe bar. I arrive before anyone... have a margarita. A good starter drink. Margaritas have lime juice which is fortified with vitamins. The definition of "fortified" according to Merriam-Webster is "to make stronger or more secure" so lime juice is the perfect liquid to begin the evening. Tequila helps too, I've heard.

20 minutes pass and I'm partially numb already. No one can hurt you if your feelings are dead. Soon a huge crowd of familiar faces forms... Scott, Sal, Dan. We drink and catch up... all good. Dan's been lifting weights... maybe tanks. He's the size of a bull. Maybe he's eating tanks. Scott's been writing YA books. Not successfully, but doing it.

There's a big table of women having dinner. They're all familiar-looking but I couldn't place a name with a face if I had a gun to my head. They wave to us and we wave back, but for all I know, they're the Canadian Women's Curling Team. When you see your face in the mirror every day, you don't notice the slow passage of time, but when you see your high school classmates... the wrinkles, the grey sideburns... the fat necks... it's abrupt. Time is ticking away. The human body decaying.

Our batch of school buddies is growing. We're drinking, doing shots, ordering rounds... insisting on paying. Everyone drinks and insists and eventually I give up... the insisting, not the drinking. After an hour, we deem ourselves properly lubricated and go. I hop up and head across the street. I don't feel like craning my neck back, waiting to see if the blob of people I'd been with are keeping in stride with me, so I run solo.

I enter the Paramount Theater in the heart of Huntington. It's a mid-sized venue that attracts A-list comedians, B-Level musical talent and C-level cover bands that cover bands you probably wouldn't want to pay money to see even if it was the actual band itself. The marquee is emblazoned with such musical talents as the keyboard player from Styx and whatever brother, if any, remains of the Allmans. Once in a while a band like the B-52s rolls in and I'm like "awesome" but then I realize Fred Schneider is 70 and the same age as my broken uncle and I'm like "no thanks." No offense to Fred. He's wonderful. For total transparency though, I've seen Michael Bolton at the Paramount... twice! Yes, that is correct... twice. He's big in Brazil and my wife is a fan. Front row center the last time. If that's not true love, I don't know what is.

This shindig takes place in The Founder's Room, an exclusive private bar under the Paramount and it's a glorious place... rich mahogany wainscoting, lush fabric furniture, exposed brick walls, cozy yet huge. Illuminated by a variety of Tiffany-style lamps and stained-glass insets. Imagine a group of wealthy New Orleans hippies found an old Irish speak-easy and redecorated while tripping on high-powered weed and reclaimed HGTV ideas.

  I stop at the velvet rope to check in. We're *that* fancy of a class. Velvet rope fancy. There's always a grand sense of satisfaction about giving your name at the velvet rope and receiving the nod that "Yes, you *are* allowed in here, peasant." Another stop at the coat check and I press a 'HELLO, my name is...' sticker to my chest. I write A.J. in giant letters. First person I meet, who's also applying a 'HELLO' sticker, is Melissa. No clue who she is. I tell her that. She straight-up tells me she has no clue who I am. We laugh. My kind of person. Perfect way to start the night! She's Greg's wife, the guy who actually got us into the Founder's Room. I know Greg... didn't know he was even married. Guess I don't know Greg that well. I carefully stroll down the darkened mineshaft hall. A bouncer jokes that I look great after all these years. I laugh even though I know he'll say it 75 more times to others. I continue towards the light and enter the sparkling room. It's on like a cocaine-induced speed dating session... stuffing 10 to 30 years of memories and updates into four hour cram-fest. I'm immediately hugging, kissing, hand-clasping and back slapping... sounds like the percussion section of a Bobby McFerrin concert.

  I drink like a fish. Moscow Mules and light beers that continue to help lubricate the process. I even dance, which seemed like a completely excellent idea at the time. Some reiteration of pop-locking, an 80s Hip Hop dance staple and go-to move for white dudes reared on reruns of *What's Happening!!*, a 70s TV classic where the main character, Rerun, pop-locked his way into our hearts. Lots of group selfies, which end up on Facebook. I'm holding the hammered copper Moscow Mule mug in every shot. Everyone else has a mug or glass... filled with wine, beer... whatever it took to ease the pain. Everyone looks amazing... the same as they did in school, just greyer. It's Summer so everyone is tanned and fresh. Even the black people look tanned. Perhaps the fat and ugly decided not to show. Why would they? This is a glamour competition in so many ways. No one wants to go in trumpeting a minimum wage job and a beer belly that enters the room before your face.

    Through the night, I kept falling into one person's gravitational pull without even trying. My friend Meredith Fudge. Meredith was, and still is radiant and magnetic... a human sunflower... and I was madly in love with her in school. But truth be told, so was everyone else. With her chestnut hair and big brown eyes, she still looks the same.

    She was on the fence about coming to the reunion but pulled the trigger on a last-minute ticket just like I did, before the deadline made it impossible to come at all. We spent a good chunk of the night laughing and catching up. She lives in the next town over, married with a daughter. But we don't cross paths. A town over but might as well be a continent over.

    Back in my senior year of high school, I let one of my art teachers look through my personal art journals for a class grade. I knew he was captivated by the drawings, but little did I realize that he would photocopy pages, blow them up, and display them in showcases outside of the auditorium. Some of the pictures were private abstract works about Meredith and my love for her, in some cases violent and strange. In one image I had a figure with a bloody knife and the word Jim, her boyfriend at the time. Many had her name and colorful swirling painted collages. Beautiful, yes... but my personal journal images were exposed for the whole school to see... my heart and soul hanging on the walls and it was mortifying. Meredith confronted me immediately... was disturbed by it... but I told her I didn't have feelings for her like that anymore... which was true because I had a girlfriend. I had my teacher pull everything down and within a few days it was forgotten... at least in my world.

Memory pangs of that art show would still rise up years later. Sometimes I think a weaker person may have gone off the deep end ... have to leave school or maybe even consider suicide. The memory still haunts me in strange ways... especially since her boyfriend Jim would die a few years later in a tragic helicopter accident. A death she's never gotten over.

•••

A swift four hours later, we are forced to leave the Founder's Room by the disgruntled staff... a dour combo of bartenders, bar backs and bouncers. They form a wall of disapproving frowns, crossed arms and impatient finger taps. One guy looks borderline violent. If they were a band, their new hit single would've been '*Exit Only*' following hot on the heels of their first hit '*You don't have to Go Home, But You*

Can't Stay Here.' Minutes before, the staff had been accommodating, charming, even jovial. But once the time expired on the rental space, their spirits plummeted faster than a falling star. So, we scattered into the night, swapping potential destinations and comparing notes. Huntington has about 30 bars, so throw a rock and you'll hit a rocks glass.

    I helped the inebriated into Ubers and waved goodbye. I planned to be sensible and go home at a decent time... like some kind of lame-ass. But something happened on the serene stroll to my car in a grocery store parking lot... I felt alone. I had that high school pang that I was missing out on something. The big party that mom and dad wouldn't let me go to. After a battle of will, I decided to meet everyone at the after-party at Greg and Melissa's in Huntington Bay... down the road from Carl's parents.

    Arriving, I was amazed at the house set on the sweeping property. A towering glass and wood mansion. Stunningly lit. Gleaming in my vodka-soaked eyes like an *Architectural Digest* spread. I followed the murmur over the backyard hill, past the garage and found the group drinking and chatting around the pool house, which was larger than my actual house. What did Greg do for a living? I wasn't sure, but I picture Greg standing inside a giant bank safe. One of those glimmering mechanical beasts -- the open rotund door, exposing golden clockwork gears and sprockets that finger out into their security holes with stunning precision and thunderous clangs.

    There were a few clusters happening. Some were huddled around the flicker of the fire pit. Others were nestled against the bar. A chain of people were crookedly poised along a wooden bench like they're preparing to enter a drunken baseball game. I spotted Meredith cordially chatting with someone, so I slid up to her. Billy Campion joins us, my old friend and workmate. His once full-faced, rockstar Irish looks, now more gaunt and ashen. The Schmitz and Campion clans have been intertwined for 60 years. Bill's oldest brother and my Uncle Paul were friends and bandmates as kids. We discuss addiction, sobriety and the creative process. Bill's voice is a husky squeak from years of bleating into a microphone with his group The Bogmen. Billy and I eventually tackle a box of cold fried chicken.

    I chatted for a few hours till I deemed myself undesirable, then spun around and said goodbye to anyone interested in hearing it, but no one was paying attention... everyone yapping aimlessly or fighting through alcohol poisoning. Brad, who'd been wringing his hands like a man who can hear his wife in his head say "You better not stay out all night" pulled an Irish goodbye and quick-stepped it out of there with me. We're ushered off by a glowering Greg who displayed two middle fingers -- one for each of us.

    Brad explained in the car that Greg expected us to stay till dawn. I fired up the Honda and Carl, who pulled a giant cooler of iced beers from his parents' house, shuffled up next to Brad and tapped on the window. Unfortunately, the passenger window doesn't go down, one of the Honda's many specialized features. We're forced to explain to Carl that we're totally lame between the headrests while he slants his head through the childproof back window.

    We drove to Brad's 'hood. His neighbor's entire house had been sadly bagged and tossed to the curb... stacks of furniture, black bags and piles of unidentified collateral. Divorce. An ugly one. The children, Russell in particular, who I played with in my youth, were responsible for emptying the place before the sheriff came to toss them out. Brad had helped, spending precious vacation time bailing out his old neighbor by stuffing furniture into his parent's garage.

Brad and I bro-hug as he climbed out. I believe I was planning on saying "Don't be a stranger" but I belched out something less understandable like… "If you're a stranger and you're here in town, come by with a Hi and…." and then I trailed off into silence to stop the pain. If I'd simply channeled Jim Morrison and sang "people are strange, when you're a stranger, people are ugly, when you're alone" it wouldn't have been any less confusing.

This was concrete proof that I departed the party at the right time. My brain was shutting down at that point. Brad was one of my earliest childhood friends when we met in kindergarten. It was appropriate that he'd be the last person from the reunion I'd see. A bookend to a school-life from long ago.

My house is milliseconds from Brad's parents. I get home before the sun comes up. Our bird Zen, who's not been covered with a blanket, judges me with a stink-eyed stare. I drink water and crunch a few potato chips before hauling my buzzing nervous system into the cool, air-conditioned bed.

I'm already pondering if I'll go to the 40th reunion and what excuses I can make for not remembering names: I was hit in the face by a line-drive at Yankee Stadium, which shook my Corpus Callosum loose. That sounds Latin and I may be forced to explain why I can remember complicated foreign brain terminology, but not the name Bob. Better yet... mistaking a cup of molasses for whiskey, I shot it down the back of my throat, choked, and cut off my air supply, causing damage to my hippocampus. That sparks images of large semi-aquatic mammals playing Frisbee on the college quad. That alone could carry into a conversation I don't want to be part of. So perhaps it's best to be truthful... I'm old and I simply don't give a shit. How's that excuse?

BUGGIN' OUT

6

TO QUEBEC
AND BEC AGAIN

Because we have a nice end-of-summer vacation road trip coming, my wife insists I take the car to the shop to be aligned. At high speeds it shakes like a Magic Fingers mattress at a cheap motel.

"What car doesn't?" I plead.

It's not a convincing argument. I've put it off for a year because I know, as God made little green apples, the mechanic is going to find an expensive problem. It's a feeling of dread. A storm cloud. I have a staggering history of shitty car problems, so why would this be different? Going in for a $100 oil change? The mechanic will find that your car needs an entire engine replacement... $9,000,000! So I've been reluctant.

The first car I ever had was a hand-me-down from my sister... a black '79 Plymouth Horizon that was similar in style and safety to a vintage ski gondola. It made the laughable Ford Gremlin look downright aerodynamic. Caroline drove the thing a million miles until the panels rattled like cowboy chaps on a bucking bronco. She handed me the keys and sped away in her new white T-topped Chevy Monte Carlo with red interior... her Farrah Fawcett hair flipping in the wind as the cool sounds of Def Leppard wafted into the sunset.

Before I gave the dreaded Horizon one spin, my father magically swapped it with his friend's orange '74 Mercury Capri because his cleaning lady couldn't drive a stick shift. I didn't argue... it was a massive upgrade on my side. The Capri was borderline stylish. I drove it constantly for two weeks when it died in the driveway on a scorching hot morning on my way to summer school. Kaput. The End. Two weeks after that I was informed that the Horizon had caught fire and burned to a blackened shell on the side of the highway. So, I guess I made out OK on the deal.

So, I take the Honda to the alignment place at the crack of dawn. Should be all smooth. Just an alignment... right? My friend Stephen, who drives me to work, assures me it's going to be fine. I don't believe him.

The mechanic calls me at noon and I can sense it. After a hard-to-read "hello," he pauses like a doctor might do before running down an itemized list of maladies I'll need to cure. He huffed, which is a sure sign of terrible news. It needs new breaks and a shitload of rods and springs and other mechanical nomenclature I don't understand. Price tag: $1,100. He seems genuinely sorry to break the news, which is unusual for a person in a for-profit business, but he's obviously seen the Honda and has taken it for a diagnosis test drive and knows that no one in their right mind would want to dump a grand into the stupid piece of shit. It hurts. It cuts into the savings. It cuts into the contingency. Even the emergency fund is in a state of emergency. I contemplate it briefly... "How important are brakes on a car anyway?" It's a fleeting thought. I sigh in deep resignation and give him the blessing to rod-and-spring it.

In the back of my mind, I think about the ring. The diamond ring I've been paying off to give to my wife for our ten-year wedding anniversary. It's right around the corner. November 27th. 2019. It's been an absurdly long payment process. Too long. Almost a year. I'm afraid they'll put it back in the case and say, "Times up!" Like a "Price is Right" game. "Sorry you missed out on the ring, but here's a lifetime supply of Rice-a-Roni."

Rita deserves it and I want to pay it off, but we have to pay for stuff like food and insurance. And, after all, it's a secret. She asks me for something arbitrary like a chandelier and I squeeze my eyes shut in anger. Even necessities like laundry detergent or bikini wax are met with conflict as I think about the ring payment in my head... and then my mouth says something stupid like "Do we really need that?" Rococo chandeliers are debatable. Laundry detergent... not so much. She doesn't reply. It's a look of disappointment she gives me. Sometimes even a sanity check... a deep look into my eyes to see if they're crossed... or if there's a soul inside. Yes, if I don't want to smell like a caveman at the office or have her look like a caveman between the legs, then some of these purchases make sense.

I'm in over my head. I know the diamond market is fixed and I'm mentally a creature of the hippie mindset, yet hosted in the body of a yuppie. Diamond rings are ridiculous!

Let's wander the earth until we find our *own* precious rock that we can whittle with axes into a ring. Organically. Like lovers do. We have friends who got a gold ring on an archaeological find in Egypt. In terms of value it's high and in the context of love tokens it's priceless. A walkabout my office building won't provide such a similar treasure. Perhaps a metal detector and a sifting basket at Robert Moses State Park beach a few miles south could produce something. But it's a lost ideal. I spend my countless days in an office and the place down the street has polished rocks for sale already. I'll buy one of theirs. I'm in the process already.

•••

At the tail end of a minor lung infection, I pack up half our house and jam it into the newly springed-and-rodded Honda CRV for an epic family road trip, which includes a cooler packed with ice to transport a yellow Carvel Minion ice cream cake to my cousin Lauren, who has professed a love of Carvel ice cream in the past. The Honda brakes are new and there's fresh oil in the engine. Everything else is a crapshoot. If it dies on the road, we'll eat ice cream until we're rescued by the banjo-plucking woodsmen from *Deliverance*. They'll demand anal penetration for their entire brood until every gap-toothed cousin is completely satisfied.

Leaving Long Island, we visit Lauren and her family in Johnson Vermont, just north of Stowe, waaaaaay up at the top of the Green Mountain State. We arrive just as a storm is leaving which is serendipitous, but gives Vermont its lowest summer night temperatures in a decade: 45 degrees. We're sleeping in a tent in their yard... fun if you're roughing it. Not fun when you're still fighting liquid-y lungs. My cousin informed me a few days prior that bears were roaming their yard, eating from the garbage cans. I picture it like a cartoon, the bears holding the garbage can lids like buffet plates, carefully selecting items with tongs. I tried to paint more humorous images to my wife: ones where a bear might use a bony fish as a comb or peck the corn off the cob like a vintage typewriter. I ran the situation by my wife, but she pictured it differently: People screaming and dragged by their feet into the woods.

Eventually she shrugged it off. A trouper for sure! Ready to camp. I may have sold her on the fact that they were most likely black bears and not grizzly bears -- black bears being one step up from puppy dogs that enjoy belly rubs, and not the Godzilla-like Grizzly, which could tear a man's arm off with its roar.

The weekend is a delight and the mountain air is medicinal. The Minion cake makes it, but its white eye slides off the yellow frosting, leaving something resembling a melted street sign. Stowe is a wonderful town. High-end skiing sophistication façade masking a hippie-beaded green mountain mentality... but buried deeper still, in the depth of reality... the poorest of the poor stuffed into the cracks. Vermont has some of the highest poverty in the country and you discover the blight between the gilded-lettered rustic signage and pine trees.

Stowe in summer is a shade less busy than Stowe in winter, but still pretty busy. Biking, hiking, wandering and drinking... and of course, tourist trap shopping. If you're like me and already grumbling about laundry detergent, $25 moose refrigerator magnets that say *Stowe* will not bring you an inch closer to Shangri-La. But playing bocce ball in the yard, tossing a frisbee in the sun, and downing some local beer is as close as I can get to Shangri-La. It's good enough. Campfire nirvana... S'mores, local beer, bar-b-que and s'more local beer. After two days of freezing our asses off and listening for bears, we break it all down, hop in the car, and head to the Canadian border.

As we drive, the countryside becomes sparser, the trees grow taller, greyer. Like totems. Mystical old men of the wilderness. I feel like Jack Torrance at the beginning of *The Shining*, riding with Hobbits as we approach Mordor... half-expecting a passageway of fire to get us through the other side... a feeling of dread. But maybe that's how I approach everything now. Sort of like a visit to the DMV. Stoic one might say. Everything will go to hell in a handbasket. But when it doesn't, it's a wonderful relief.

I assumed the border crossing would be more complicated: a heel-clicking Nazi with jetted leather glove barking, "Paperz pleaze." In this day and age, I pretty much assume I'll be ripped from the car, slammed on the hood and cavity-searched while a family from Nebraska watches terrified through their Winnebago windows. But luckily, there are just a few questions at the booth, a request that my wife remove her sunglasses, and up to Quebec City we go.

We reach Quebec City, much like Northern Vermont, at the tail end of a rainstorm, leaving the city sunny-fresh and cool. And it's gorgeous! A European city if there ever was one. An hour's drive from our American border. The food is great, the people are great, the architecture is great... the weather is great. It's a wonderful time. New town, old town.... The whole town. We walk the city up and down till we drop. It's like an extension of Paris, except the people aren't rude. I know there's a myth that the French hate Americans, but it's not true. The French hate everyone equally.

After three days of bus tours, local food and mingling with the locals, we're on the road to Montreal. We have one afternoon walking the city. Again, another lovely city. We walk as much as we can. It's eerily similar to New York. Like someone tossed one part Brooklyn and two parts lower Manhattan Financial District into a pot and sprinkled in a touch of Paris. We saw as much as we could. The hotel suggested taking a main avenue, but failed to mention half the city is under construction, so we marched through a series of wooden, netted tunnels as jackhammers rumbled our chests. We order room service and dip in the hotel pool. The next day on the road, we take the final stretch back to America. Again, I'm positive this time we'll be cavity-searched, but I'm not as nervous for myself as I am for my wife... the Brazilian foreigner! So, if anyone is getting cavity-searched, it's her. But there's nary a problem and we cross the border into New York and head south to the lovely city of Syracuse.

More specifically, Syracuse University campus. My alma mater. The 'ol college stomping grounds. The place where I honed my abilities to scribble complicated bearded cartoons into notebooks and grasp some form of skill and education as to not be a completely useless humanoid in the real world. Having narrowly escaped high school... graduated, one might say, based solely on twisted doodles in sketch books,

I jumped into college. I spent 1990 at C.W. Post University on Long Island, then transferred to Syracuse University. I did all the typical school things kids do at school. Maybe you've been there yourself. House parties, keg stands, bands in the attic... dropping acid in snowstorms. Typical stuff.

Syracuse got a ridiculous amount of snow. One time we got four feet in one day. That's not an exaggeration. After the city plowed the streets, there were eight-foot snow walls everywhere. We were literally living in a maze. I studied advertising. It takes a special level of douche bag to enter the field. A prerequisite is to see at what decibel level you can drip sarcasm. A master classman can do it without words... a mime of derision. Top-level execs can lay waste with the curl of the mouth. I didn't connect with a soul in the department. I gravitated to the film people. Starred in all their student films. Made a few films of my own. Studied film history.

The campus was empty when we arrived, but there'd be 20,000 students blasting through in less than a week for the fall semester. Although the hotel clerk presented this information to us with a sense of pending doom, his pin-straight posture and glistening smile betrayed the fact that he'd be dizzy with satisfaction in knowing he was an early part of the Syracuse University greeting process. "That nice desk clerk with the sharp haircut. The guy who gave us the card key." High school is a place you're dying to leave immediately. College is a place you're dying to stay in forever. At least in terms of ideals. Tuition is another matter.

We walked the entire campus. First time I'd been back in 25 years. When the air is too warm for the moisture to produce back-breaking mountains of snow, it reconstitutes itself as stifling, ass-quagmire levels of humidity. We pop into old buildings like the churchy Crouse Building and visit classrooms where I once sat. The campus hadn't really changed... and that was good.

Standing before the ratty tinderbox at 741 Livingston Street, I'm stunned to see my old house hasn't crumbled to the ground in a smoking heap. Considering it's made of dry, 100-year-old lumber and insulated with newspaper, it somehow survived ten thousand glowing marijuana embers. I suppose they don't make 'em like they used to. Houses or anything. Maybe students. I was tempted to knock on the door and see if my old bed was still there, but I thought better of it... it's gone. But probably not gone is Fred, the rat we used in a film called *Bloodvisions* that eventually escaped. Ate right through his plastic house... his lineage is probably still living in the attic where I played the drums.

Later we hop in the Honda to cover more ground. Getting to the little bars, shops and nooks I used to hit when I had my college car. Ironically, a beat-up yet dependable Honda. Then the rain comes. Crashes down in buckets. Having snuck through the back end of two storms, one finally caught up to us. Through the cascading sheets of blurry water, I point out the places we used to "hang out." Since my son and wife are in the car, I refrain from dredging up the hilarious memories of stumbling home smashed, vomit breath and the regretful hookups with cigarette-stained girls.

Then we stop by an old rental apartment. The house is smaller than I remember. The apartment side entrance is tiny and super-close to the road. I thought it was much further back. Like 50 feet. But it's more like eight.

Reverend Norman W. Haight was our landlord and occupied the space next door. He seemed like Humpty Dumpty – a few doctors' visits after his great fall. He moved so gingerly and spoke so softly, we all feared high-decibel noises would shatter his glued pieces. We learned he *did* have a great fall, on the unforgiving Syracuse snow. His veiny head bulged like a mad scientist diverting all his powers to his cranium, forsaking the body. Kevin Sherwood and I lived there our senior year. Norman was thrilled when we offered to paint the place if he bought the supplies, but was horrified when I painted my room whore-house burgundy and we plastered the living room with aluminum foil faces and coated them in something resembling mustard.

As we leave, I look around again. If a 50-foot yard is actually eight feet, what else is my memory betraying? It gets complicated. I'm as big as I've been since I was 18, but was my mind smaller then? My vision? My interpretation of the world? My ability to judge distance and length in feet? Maybe the confusing times were more fun? Were the hard times more forging? What if I had dropped less acid back then and tried peyote?

Then a feeling creeps up on me. What else did I misperceive? In high school I felt like a dripping nerd. Maybe I was cooler than I thought. People at my high school reunion told me I was cool. Dana, a girl I had a crush on since 7th grade told me she was madly in love with me in school. I was floored. My mind whirled. I was painfully quirky in school... an outsider in some circles, cool in others. Interesting in one clique... a fucking faggot in other cliques. Perception is from where you're viewing it... from which lens. Now, or in retrospect. It's hard to fathom. Was life a lie or was I simply not paying attention? What could I have done with that information then? I could have been a different human! People thought I was cool and the girl I loved actually loved me back. I missed an alternate universe where I lived a perfect teenage life. If I had tried out for quarterback of the football team and made it, I may have been the All-American boy. Except while others actually threw a football, I was making eyeglasses in the cafeteria out of plastic forks and a lighter.

It seems simple communication could have torn down these walls and made the path of life less confusing. But that's 20/20 hindsight. Life is supposed to be confusing. My path was set. I was who I was. I got through high school and college doing the things I did. I suppose doubt is always in play. Could I have studied harder? What if I asked *that* girl out on a date? What If I went on this road instead of that? Literally and figuratively. Why am I asking so many questions? These thoughts washed over me. Going back in time is a terrible idea. It plants the seed of doubt. It adds another 'What-If?' to an already series of doubts about the roads not taken. It's human nature to regret... preventable if you simply march on.

Since half of Syracuse is shut down, waiting for the parade of students to fire the engines of business, we eat in the beige hotel restaurant. It's in the middle of a makeover, so the modern eating area clashes jarringly with a 1977 Beefsteak Charlie's bar... its stained-glass chandeliers and green wallpaper inviting any lost Scotsman to enjoy a rugby match and a pint.

The next day the sun is out. We're exhausted. We

spent a week on the road. We get in the Honda and drive back to Long Island. We've eaten out every night and we've walked a million miles. Even though the Honda has been blessed with all sorts of new struts and gears, it rides like a wooden toboggan over a hill of paving stones. But she makes it back... carrying us all home in one piece, where we order Chinese food and crash hard... into our own wonderful, cozy beds.

7

CONDIMENTS, CONDITIONERS AND COFFEE

The world is in serious need of a new condiment. Where is it already? Why hasn't anyone working in the experimental food recipe industry invented a new one yet? All these big companies like Kraft and Heinz and even fast food chains like McDonalds are always creating new recipes and flavor combinations. So why isn't there a new condiment?

Mayonnaise has been around for hundreds of years. So has that 84-ounce jar of mayo in your refrigerator. Mayo is a spastic concoction of eggs and whipped oil and vinegar. I like mayo. But what psycho first whipped up that bastardized batch of funkiness? What was he trying to make in the first place? Wagon wheel grease?

Then we have ketchup. Mashed tomatoes and vinegar (a constant in these things) stewed with sugar and salt. Seems simple, yet there's no variation on this either. You'd think that taking anything and mashing it into a paste with vinegar would work, but apparently not, as nothing has been invented yet that tickles our palates.

Mustard is a plant seed. How the hell did this one come about? Millions smear this strange neon yellow seed on hot dogs and sandwiches every day, yet no one thinks as to why. Has there been no further advancement in the seed industry to percolate our taste interests? I find it hard to believe. Some company makes something called Baconnaise. It's a bacon-based mayonnaise. Might as well call it massive coronary in a jar. Even for someone who gravitates towards food that's really shitty for me, Baconnaise makes my aorta scream in terror. In Great Britain, they use HP sauce, which they affectionately refer to as brown sauce. Again, it's vinegar based and is really just a ketchup-like product on steroids. Sort of like fermented gravy in a bottle, yet it's meat-free. Sounds unappetizing, I know, but it's actually pretty good.

We have all kinds of jellies and jams and pickle relish, hot sauce, taco sauce, steak sauce, barbeque sauce, soy sauce, Worcestershire sauce, teriyaki sauce, duck sauce, sweet & sour sauce, hollandaise sauce, béarnaise sauce, tartar sauce, cranberry sauce and pestos and salsas and salad dressings of all varieties. Yet none have made a permanent place on the essential condiment rack that litter the food courts as far as I can see. Have you ever seen a waitress come to your table with one of those metal carry racks filled with condiments for your meal and seen something new?

No! It's a condiment dilemma!

Salt and pepper is fine and dandy, and they're especially charming when they appear in those little Corona Beer bottles with plastic caps with holes punched in them. But salt and pepper has been around since the dinosaur age and let's face it, they're not colorful or liquidy and we're not dumping it on our burgers. They're flavor enhancers and can barely be considered condiments. They're more like elements.

Soy sauce has gotten a bit more popular in the United States. It seems to be more commonplace on the table, but that may be due to the popularity of Asian foods. Chinese has been huge for years and sushi, Thai, Korean and Vietnamese are becoming more popular dinner choices all the time. But soy sauce isn't really a condiment either. It's really just a liquid salt.

These days, people make their own condiments. They mash up fruit and veggies and call it chutney. "Tonight, we have a mouth-watering honey-glazed pork loin with a mango chutney." Chutney's nice, but that's just glorified apple sauce. Is apple sauce a condiment? Not really. It's tasty and all, but I'm looking for the new ketchup. Where is it?

A few years ago, Heinz introduced a green ketchup to mix things up. It failed miserably. It was still ketchup, and that was probably the problem! If it was made from asparagus or eucalyptus or something, then it might have piqued an interest. But trying to get a seven-year-old to buy into the concept of a ketchup that's anything but its cheerfully bright red color they've come to love is a majorly misdirected idea. Only a stupid adult would think of something so stupid.

Miracle Whip has been riding on the coattails of mayo since the 1930's, but it's freakin' mayonnaise too! I can't tell the difference! If you're slathering a white cream on your turkey, cheese and lettuce sandwich, you're probably not noticing the subtle differences between these two fat-based spread products. Burger joints have a "secret sauce" which is usually just Russian dressing; which is actually just ketchup and mayo mixed together. But no one seems to have even made this leap in condiment technology—mixing two condiments together. Seems like it'd be easy, but I guess not. Sometimes you see the pickle relish and mustard combo thing on the store shelf, but it looks like a jar of nuclear waste. Terrible! It's almost as bad as the jar of peanut butter and jelly in the same jar. What lazy bastard invented that one?

Tartar sauce is mayo and pickle relish, basically. Has anyone actually sat in a kitchen and mixed different condiment combinations together? I mean really gone for it? Mixing four or five together to find a new sauce? If I had the time, I'd do it, I would, but I have a job. It has to be someone's job to figure this crap out! Is the President on this project? What's his personal chef doing when he's traveling around in Air Force One? Can't those White House kitchen guys knock out a few ideas? Who's paying these people? I think *we* are, that's who! I want these guys on the job right now! Have them ask the president to haul back a bunch of ponzu sauce and other stuff on Air-Force One the next time the President is bouncing around the Pacific Rim.

So that's my hope in life right now: to have the great pleasure of placing a newfangled sauce on my steaming wiener or fried meat patty. Whether it be a rich and creamy white sauce, or a spicy and tangy red sauce, or something completely new and different. I have high hopes for the chefs of the world. I truly believe they can do it. I *hope* they can do it. I think it's essential for the growth of humankind as we know it.

Maybe they will invent a black sauce or a chunky blue sauce to put on my burger and greasy deep-fried potatoes. Have we invented any new colors in the last few years?

•••

One thing that has come a long way is soap. Back when I was a kid, my mother would slap a bar of neon-orange Dial in my hand and tell me to wash up. That bar would last so long, it would sit in the soap dish and get a sickly white coating and eventually split down the middle like a beached log baking in the sun. A hundred years before that, folks would wash their hair, clothes and the side of a horse with the same bar of soap. Now we have all kinds of "soap." And I put soap in quotes because we've advanced way beyond what is considered simple washing soap these days. Now we have body butters, exfoliating body washes and dermatologist- recommended medicinal scrubs containing the essence of plant DNA gleaned from the rain forests of the earth. It's possible these things could cure cancer if given a chance. These skin cream washes contain moisturizers and scents so enticing, you'd want to smear it on toast and wash it down with a swig of all-natural conditioning shampoo. They're organic, all-natural and even have fortifying vitamins inside. It seems that they'd be better for you if you ate them, rather than rub them on your body.

Now that I'm older, I've advanced from Dial to Dove. Dove has one-quarter moisturizing cream and it does help my skin. Unfortunately, I go through Dove faster than I go through Dove ice cream bars. I need a new bar every three days and often find myself milking the tiny chip that's glued to the soap holder on my shower wall. If I'm not careful, that little sliver can slip out of my hand and go down the drain and I'm stuck washing myself with shampoo. If I collect enough of the remaining soap chips, I can wad three or four into one mini-bar that lasts me a few days longer.

Shampoo has evolved as well. They include nut extracts and vitamins and all sorts of botanical things, so you're almost convinced your hair is mending itself with some sort of magic potion. The TV commercials convince you as well. They have animated diagraphs of split ends melding together like a salamander growing a new tail. The women on the commercials seem so pleased that they toss their giant manes of hair around in slow motion, their locks bouncing with a shine usually reserved for sports cars after a Simonizing. Then you are instructed to use a fortifying conditioner because it's paired with the shampoo. If you follow the instructions carefully, washing your hair can take hours.

Soap for all household uses has advanced in technology as well. Dish soap has antibacterial natures, laundry detergent does just about everything but fold your clothes, and household cleaners can strip the paint off the wall if not used properly. These cleaning products use the power of oxygen as well as little bubbles that provide the elbow grease for you. These bottles combine things like bleach and ammonia, which back in the day would explode in your face, but somehow seems to work together today. They're all sold to you by bearded guys who scream at you through the TV, begging you not to miss out on the deal. These deals are usually so good they give you two, plus a bizarre scraper/chopper thing that didn't seem to make it on its own as a viable TV product.

If you go to any pharmacy, especially a bigger one,

there's about 10,000 different shampoos and soaps on the shelf. There's more choices than microbrews and wines combined. Where do you even begin to start? It seems like half are named after a person. Sally Herbal...blah blah or Mitchell Something-or-other. Apparently there are shampoo superstars coming up the ranks faster than a reality show about food/fashion/models and they're all releasing their amazing locks elixir, which I'm sure is probably just like the other 999 bottles of soap on the shelf. Still, it's fun to stare at all the colors. It tends to be mesmerizing.

Way back when, soaps and shampoos were basically rendered fat. The difference between a bar soap and a candlestick depended on where you kept it in your house. Today, most kids haven't even seen a candle. Modern-day candles have so many scents in them, kids may be tempted to wash with them if they aren't under proper supervision.

I once had dandruff so bad, my dermatologist gave me a prescription for shampoo that recommended that I remove my jewelry before using it. That can't be a good sign. What's in that stuff — silver polish? It looked more like Liquid Drano than the cool, seafoam green of Head and Shoulders. Still, the stuff worked and my dandruff was cured -- although there's probably a school of fish swimming around the Atlantic somewhere, each with three eyes and the scent of Febreze.

My wife got a basket of fine soaps for Christmas and some of the soap bars had seeds in them. Actual fruit plant seeds! She said one was from a Brazilian fruit that was very rare. I used it in the shower and I swear I felt fantastic afterwards -- like someone had bathed me in liquid sunshine and patted me dry with flower petals. Bar soaps are becoming a thing of the past, though. Most people use liquid soaps and scrub with a loofah. Sometimes I get in the shower and there's so many scrubbers, sponges and bottles, I feel like I'm in a science lab. The art of getting clean is kind of expensive, but it's better than walking around with your pores clogged with soap gunk. A lot of soaps and shampoos claim not to test on animals, and that's a fine thing, but what are they testing them on now? Are there people out there being paid handsomely to risk looking horrible? I would imagine a soap product going terribly wrong may be even more problematic than one that ripped up your stomach or gave you anal leakage. Actually, now that I write that out, I feel confident a skin rash may be more tolerable than an asshole that doesn't function correctly.

The days of soap on a rope may be numbered. They're experimenting these days with cleaning things by sound waves. That's nice. It could possibly cause hearing damage, but you'll be clean. Image going to a concert and leaving cleaner than when you entered the stadium... It's possible! I once knew a guy who rubbed a shiny rock under his arms instead of deodorant and it actually worked. He smelled just fine. Not sure how that technology works, but I think I'll stick to a nice bar of Dial soap and scalding hot water to eliminate odors before I risk going outside under the mysterious power of crystals.

•••

Coffee has evolved way beyond what many people thought it'd be a hundred years ago. Catch any 40s noir film, and you'll see a man saunter into a diner, snap the rain off his jacket with the yank of his collar and order a rare steak with black coffee. Back then they ate everything with black coffee: tuna sandwiches, oniony meatloaves and Cobb salads, all topped off with a steaming cup of rich, black coffee.

I'm not sure the marriage of coffee and cream materialized until the mid-Sixties. Maybe around the time mixed marriages were legalized. Might be related, I don't know. But coffee drinks have advanced way beyond the norm. I'm a big fan of iced coffee. In the summertime, I can drain three in a row and have coffee jitters so intense, I have to do a few laps around the block just to stop my hands from shaking. But all the creamy elixirs and flavored potions that go into iced coffee drinks is stupefying. And they're loaded with belly-blasting calories too.

If you've ever been to a Starbucks, you'll notice a lengthy line that serpentines around the interior like a 1929 bread line. The reason for this phenomenon is the absurdly huge frozen coffee drinks that people order with twelve ingredients in them. Every time I go into a Starbucks, there's a woman in front of me ordering an iced coffee drink that is so complicated, my eyes glaze over. The barrister accepts the order with a slide ruler and a NASA handbook. It takes her six minutes to order the damn thing and it has so much sugar, cream and drizzles in it, I'm not sure it qualifies as a coffee drink. I'm not sure it qualifies as a drink! It usually has to be consumed with a spoon. I feel like stopping her midway through the order and say "Hey, whoa, whoa, whoa! Slow down there, missy. Why don't you just snort some caffeine pills and hit the Baskin-Robbins across the street and get yourself a milk shake, for the love of Pete!" Whipped cream is a topping for children, not a cap for your coffee. Grow up.

    By the time I get to the counter to order my drink, I simply mutter "coffee" and slink off to the side. How do people even know to order half the stuff on the menu? Do they experiment with different combinations until they nail it? How long does it take to find the combination you like? A month? A year? A lifetime? Going to Starbucks is the equivalent of going to the DMV. Long lines, disgruntled staff and obnoxious people in front of me -- all for the privilege of paying $7.35 for coffee that kind of tastes like dirt. I'm pretty sure I can get the exact same coffee and service at the post office. Now there's a million places that serve coffee so you don't have to be a slave to the Starbucks chain. But many people are addicted to Starbucks. I had a co-worker who'd say, "I need my Starbucks!" Not "I need coffee" or even "I need a venti triple half-caff double espresso frapachino with caramel foam whip macchiato" -- but "I need Starbucks!" It's like when people call tissues Kleenex or any soda Coke. It's in our lexicon for god's sakes! My wife likes Starbucks, so we go, but inside I'm quietly fighting a battle of morals. If I get to the door and seven fifteen-year-olds enter before me, I turn around and leave. They'll be ordering for half the morning.

    Some people don't like iced coffee. They can only drink coffee hot and I can understand that. For those people, coffee is more than just a beverage. It's a morning ritual, a pattern, an overall feeling more than a drink. Coffee, crap, shower and go... and if anything disrupts the flow, the flow gets disrupted. Some people I know cannot function without coffee. They are literally worthless slabs of human flesh without that morning Cup o' Joe. I used to date a woman who traveled with her own automatic coffee pot for fear that she wouldn't be able to find coffee while on the road. That's addiction right there. I once met a guy who was so into coffee, he began roasting his own coffee beans in his $10,000 coffee-roasting oven he had installed in his kitchen. Of course I found this completely mind-blowing as I'd just graduated from buying store-bought coffee in a can to purchasing fresh ground coffee at the coffee shop.

    Now, I'm bit of a coffee snob. I actually drink it black. Looking at my cholesterol levels, my doctor suggested slowing down on the red meat and dairy, so I eliminated cream from my coffee. That decision probably added about three or four days onto the end of my life. Drinking coffee black leaves no room for error. Cream and sugar will disguise crappy coffee. With black, there's no forgiveness. Nothing between the silky black gold and the buds of the tongue. The first cup of coffee that I remember having was a foamy, funky mug of Taster's Choice instant coffee. I think that's as low as you can go in the coffee-consuming totem pole. The freeze-dried jar of brown gravel bits that I yanked from my parent's kitchen cabinet was probably a few years old at the time. It was the emergency coffee they kept for unannounced guests, except they usually ended up drinking scotch. And the taste? About one level up from warm horse-piss. Eventually, I moved up to a 50¢ cup of coffee at the deli en route to my house-painting job. Usually that was being poured down my gullet over a sloppy egg sandwich, so the coffee quality was irrelevant to the cheese, bacon and egg combo I was hammering down my throat.

When I worked in midtown Manhattan, my only option was to slug it out with 500 people every morning in a shoebox-sized Starbucks to get my overpriced coffee that tasted like Scottish hillside mulch. The office I worked in had a single-serving insta-brew coffee maker in the kitchenette, but those had varying levels of quality, especially if the only remaining flavor was hazelnut or jungle rich dark or some other puzzling name. Those pod and packets tend to have more variety than the shampoo and soap section at the pharmacy: French Vanilla, Espresso Bean, Donut Shop, Sumatra, Breakfast Blend, Hurricane Dark Spanish Moss Sacrificial Virgin Roast. Ethiopian, Italian, Colombian... House Blend. What's a house blend? Is that when they just mix a bunch of random coffees in a pot? "Try the house blend. Pedro accidentally dropped the Hazelnut Vanilla into the Americano. It's wonderfully rich."

One day I got a coffee maker as a gift in the mail. It wasn't for me per se, but for the person who lived in my apartment before me. I picked up the phone and tried to return it to the company, but they didn't care. I even tried to forward it to the previous renter's address, but no one seemed to want the stupid thing, so I kept it. My first official coffee maker -- in my home! It came with some high-quality coffee in silver and gold packets. When the silver and gold ran dry, I panned for coffee at the D'Agostino's across the street and struck Folger's. I got two cans because it was on sale. I got French Roast because I believed the French to be high connoisseurs of coffee and would actually be a step up from the regular Folger's, but I was mistaken. It was the same generic dirt and its only relation to France was its can tasted similar to the Eiffel Tower.

While traversing the same D'Agostino's aisles, I came across a coffee pyramid advertising two cans for the price of one. Café Bustelo. It was a coffee epiphany! Even though it was coffee in a can, the quality was better tenfold. The grounds were rich and moist, thick like potted soil and the smell was fresh. Those two cans really woke me up (no pun intended) to coffee and how good it can be. I continued my loyalty to that brand until that particular sale ran out on the 2-for-1 deal. What can I say, I was on a budget. Later, my wife told me about good Brazilian coffee. I went to my local coffee shop and ordered half a pound of Brazilian Cerrado and had it ground before my eyes. In that moment, I was hooked. There is simply nothing better than that first cup of fresh ground coffee.

My parents would grind their coffee beans every morning, but they grew tired of the work involved. Unfortunately, they stepped down from fresh ground beans all the way to a Costco oil barrel that lasts about eight months. I never wanted to get involved with the grinder because it's noisy and seems like a lot of effort to get great coffee. But going from canned to fresh ground is a huge leap. So here I am, all fancy and shit, enjoying my coffee, thinking it's the best, but it's not even close to the level it could be. I could still buy the beans and grind them myself in my home just seconds before the hot water drains over them -- coffee that is even fresher still. But then I met a guy in a business meeting who roasts his own beans in his $10,000 coffee oven and I'm officially an amateur in the coffee-consuming world.

But there's still more levels of coffee than even this guy and his $10,000 oven. He could potentially cultivate and grow his own coffee brand. When you start dabbling in farming so you can sip a cup of coffee, you've really hit the stratosphere. But there's more! He could *buy* a coffee plantation in Columbia or somewhere in South America…work with farmers and coffee experts to create the finest beans they possibly can for the best cup of coffee to drink. Then, taking coffee into the future, he could work with scientists and horticulturists about crossbreeding the two or three best coffee beans in the world to make one ultra-delicious super-bean that could blow the minds of coffee drinkers all around the planet. Maybe I've gone too far.

So, if you're out enjoying the warm, summer air and you need a little caffeine boost, by all means, order a nice iced coffee and kick-start your afternoon. If you need a little sugar blast to satisfy your sweet tooth cravings, order a cookie to go along with it, or perhaps a biscotti. But if you find yourself in a Starbucks line, ready to ramble off a laundry list of sugars and creams to dump into your "coffee drink," do everyone behind you a favor, go to the grocery store and get a pint of Ben & Jerry's ice cream and save us all the pain of being stuck on line for fifteen minutes behind you when all we want to do is go outside, get on with our day and enjoy our coffee.

8

FOOTLOCKER TREASURES
PART I

It's 2018 and I'm eating dinner with my parents at their country club, which they adore, and I... tolerate. It's all fine... I'm not a club person. Club people enjoy the finer things in life. Eighteen holes of golf and liquors aged in wooden barrels older than the Declaration of Independence. They're doctors and lawyers... puppet masters yanking the financial fabric of the planet's monetary system based solely on their egotistical whims.

Me, I'm one gnarly traffic jam away from running deep into the wilderness, never to return to civilized society again. But the food at the club is good and there's some nice people. Mostly my parents' friends and the staff. There's also the walking dead in Polo shirts. You can see it in their soul as their kids run screaming by... their eyes glazing over, staring off into the distance. They think money is a personality trait, so I don't have a lot in common with them other than the obvious... lungs, brains, stomachs, those types of things.

So, in the middle of my second beer and third plate of food, my father says I need to do something about the giant trunk of stuff in the attic. He says it like I need a haircut or "that damn leaky motorcycle in the driveway!" It's blocking access to other crap in the attic my father never looks at, so it has to go.

So I took it. And it sat in my kitchen for two days until my wife made me take it to my workshop outside. The beastly box is a strange seafoam blue with brass hinges, buffers and locks so rusted with age, it's a tetanus shot waiting to happen. It's a relic from 1964, but I inherited in 1994 when my father removed his old high school and college shit and I replaced it with my old high school and college shit. This time capsule sat in the bone-dry attic above the garage for 20 years until the country club dinner ultimatum. I took it home and it sat in the middle of my kitchen for two days until my wife begged me take it to my workshop.

In my damp, wet workshop under the kitchen, the footlocker smells like a dank basement. Moldy and tainted. I quickly sift through the wreckage. And wreckage it is. A nightmare.

I'm in the business of looking back often. I'm constantly updating my art portfolio so I can present my best work... adding, subtracting... making tough decisions. This is good, this is shit. This is relevant, this is dated... it's the business. But this archeological dig was disappointing at best and depressing at worst. Not a walk down memory lane. A tumble through the awkward years. Cringe-inducing.

I pick up the first sketch book I see. One of the many black faux leather-bound books I've used over time. Half the cover is painted white with sketches on it, which seems pointless considering there are hundreds of pages of white paper *inside* to use. It's from my sophomore year in college... brimming with endless doodles. Most of it inspired by hazed marijuana brain-spilling. Not repetitive in nature as one would attack a subject and hone the image till perfection, but repetitive in nature like slamming your head against the wall. Pages upon pages of stupid cartoon faces... repeated over and over with little to no point. Graffiti with no message. Comic strips with no punch lines. Characters with no stories. The kind of doodles you scratch into the corner of a legal pad as you yap away on the phone with your cousin in Indiana.

Triangles within triangles... circles next to circles... the circles eventually become the eyes of a cartoon, that eventually gets a face, then a beard as baroque as an American Civil War general. Technically stunted ideas with no redeeming quality. I toss the book back and slam the locker lid in anger. I decide to continue later with a different mindset. Maybe tomorrow... or 20 years.

Years ago when I began tossing items into the seafoam box, I thought it was just an act of storage – a way to keep my work and photos organized and not strewn across the floor like everything else I own. Now that time has passed, the footlocker isn't just a storage box. It's a Pandora's box. A time capsule of memories, hauntings and personality changes waiting to spring out and torture me.

I envision sliding the footlocker down my backyard slope and lighting it on fire... Viking funeral style. But now that I've cracked it open, I'm determined to go back in time and review myself... a "this was your life!" evaluation.

Humans are on a continual search for themselves and their purpose in life, but what they're really doing during the quest is inventing themselves. They Chisel away the pieces of their marble block until their true self is revealed. Part of that process is leaving the past behind, so going deep into the footlocker might be a terrible idea. I'm sure it's a terrible idea. I'll confront a lifetime of dubious choices that I walked away from long ago. Maybe a review of the past will clarify my present. Isn't looking at the stuff of your youth the magical key to unlocking life's most difficult current existential questions?

•••

When we first moved into our rental the year before, the house bestowed a housewarming gift... at least to me. Upon first arrival, I noticed a distinct smell when I entered the kitchen. Faint at first, but it grew stronger as time went on. Marijuana. I was positive as the smell lingered... a random splash in the face from time to time. But when I searched the drawers and cabinets where the smell was emanating from, it yielded nothing. Perhaps there was a secret compartment. A hidden passageway that lead to a study with giant bookshelves and a golden owl. Like the board game Clue. But every nascent nasal investigation ended in a cold case. Not even after 25 searches... like somehow it was to magically appear. Like the food in the fridge you think you missed the first eight times you stuck your nose in.

Eventually the smell was so strong, it was overwhelming. With dogged determination, I got on my knees and dug inside the lower cabinets, twisting around plumber-style... then I saw it! Stuck between the drawers above was a plastic bag. I scissored my fingers up between the woodwork and yanked it out. Lo and behold, about an ounce of fresh weed. The good shit! The people who resided there before us let one slip by. Probably cursed the world over losing it... or blamed one another for smoking it all. So, I stashed my stash in a coffee can in the workshop amongst the dead insects and loose screws.

    I resurrected my old one-hitter and partook in a puff before digging into the footlocker. Nothing says stable walk down memory lane like anxiety-induced weed tokes and childhood confrontation. Why not get erratically high and have a talk with 16-year-old you? Sure to send you screaming into the night. A good chunk of this stuff was created on marijuana, so why not get in the same headspace? After an hour of cleaning the workshop and avoiding confrontation, I stare at the pile of the past. All of it a dirty, dented, musty lump of nostalgia. I'm doing a complete soul cleansing... a total past life purge. I channel my inner Indiana Jones... even though I'm looking more like his dad, Henry Jones, and awaken the ghosts of my past.

    Three days after I started, I flop the lid open again and just go at it. Decades of my graphics work printed on high-quality paper when portfolios were presented in person and not sent into the hellish void of the internet. Ads for History Channel, posters for HBO. Pamphlets, promotional pieces, brochures, menus... all garbage. Most of it now in digital form, so I toss it all into the thick black contractor garbage bag. It's double-lined so I can't tear it open and take it all back.

    I pull stacks upon stacks of papers... a dead forest of papers that include, schematics, drawings, designs and color notes involving endless amounts of Christmas tabletop toys for our biggest client in 1999, Mr. Christmas. Most of it dated before it hit the shelves, making portions of the portfolio feel like a relic from 1958. Mr. Christmas was a million-dollar account that was procured and nurtured by my boss, Howard, like one might watch over the famous golden goose.

    Run with clockwork precision, Mr. Christmas was owned and operated by Terry Hermanson, a visionary Jewish businessman with the face and charm of a petrified totem pole. I imagined the company name was born from a heated argument over territorial Christmas selling spots in 1950, another Jewish businessman shouting at the company's founder, Merril Hermanson "You don't know spit about Christmas!" and Merril firing back across a row of stunned cronies "I don't know anything about Christmas? I'm MR. CHRISTMAS!" But when I pressed Terry about the genesis of the name while serving him coffee one morning, he growled "I don't know, my father came up with it." I believe that was the longest conversation I ever had with him.

    One of the perks of that job was doing research. Our office was in Union Square, a skip across the street to a giant three-floor Toys R Us. I'd be asked to go purchase toys and return with an armful of glittering boxes, cooing dolls and foil-packaged action figures. Some I was able to keep after the research was over... some still in the desired sealed boxes. But taking fresh toys and dissecting them like lab frogs always left me with a tinge of regret. The most egregious being the time Terry came bearing an extremely rare tin Mickey Mouse Roller Coaster toy from the late 1940s that he left in our office... the $3,000 price tag still flapping in the breeze. The giant set ran little carts, occupied by Disney's most recognizable clubmates, around a twisty, multi-tiered mini amusement park, which would delight even the most cold-hearted grump. After we'd studied the set and had drawn all the necessary pictures and schematics, I returned the following morning to find Mickey, Donald and Goofy had been shipped to Hong Kong where our Chinese builders completely dismantled the coaster into tiny, indistinguishable fragments. Value: $0. I was nearly inconsolable. Looking at the schematic in my hands, I'm crestfallen all over again. Sure, we made a fairly decent Santa roller coaster version, but that Mickey coaster was a piece of history and we trashed in like a cheap beer can.

Terry and Howard pumped out endless amounts of honking cars, chiming music boxes, ringing carousels and buzzing light ornaments... most donning the image of our sacred father, Santa Claus and his winking, cherub-faced, bowl full of jelly. All of the stuff good-looking and charming... none of it meant to last. Especially if a child so much as breathed on it, let alone played with it. Howard was an inspiration for our artist Dan in the design department as Howie was similar in size, shape and roundness to Old Saint Nick himself. His face a winking, cherry-nosed, cherub-like incarnation of the North Pole resident, yet blessed with a head of hair as thick, lush and dark as a military shoeshine brush.

At the bottom of the paper pile, under the "Nutcracker Suite," a rotating tabletop showpiece that displayed the play in four acts, is a letter of recommendation from Howard. The letter says I had more potential than anyone he ever saw and should be hired yesterday, if not sooner. I never used that letter. He wrote it to ease his guilt over firing me.

After another puff, I hit a box of letters and photos. The deteriorating wine box looks like it was rescued from an earthquake. It's been nursed back to health multiple times with layers of dry, crumbling shipping tape. Inside is 52 pickup times a thousand. Every photo cluster from every decade has been blended like a cocktail. Each snapshot launching me to another place and time. Wormhole whiplash. Everything shuffled together with postcards from people who'd traveled the world and dropped me a line. I pluck papers out, peel things off one another... like a plate of sloppy nachos... strategically pulling apart and twisting the yellowing notes, the decaying papers and crumpled images. Things that once stuck to the doors and walls of my apartments with scotch tape are now taped to other things with Scotch tape. Photos of Clint Eastwood chomping a thin cigar, Malcolm X, Bruce Lee, Abbey Road, Joan Miro, ... a visual library of everything I was into at the time. Goopy ephemera sandwiches.

There's a mélange of rejection letters. Rejection letters from film festivals, rejection letters from screenplay contests. A letter from a screenplay contest with a personal note saying how much they liked my Film Noir treatment of the material, although upon closer inspection, it's a ready-made letter forged to LOOK like it was newly hand-written. Apparently, they got so many noir screenplays, they had an off-the-rack letter to dump in the mail... probably 20 ready-made categories to pluck and ship. "We really enjoyed your SCIENCE FICTION screenplay, we really liked how you developed the

ALIENS."

I unfold a beautifully hand-illustrated letter from my first college art teacher, Carrie with caricature sketches of her daily life. She thanked me for coming to her art show in Kew Gardens, the only student of hers who did... telling me she always knew I'd be special. Whether that sentiment was genuine because she actually felt that way or because I'd shown up, I'm unsure. Not only do I not remember going to the show, I'm pretty sure I've never been to Kew Gardens.

Then, I reluctantly crack some letters. Slip them from their browning envelopes. The mix of handwritings, stamp cancels from different cities... different states. Spain, Iraq, San Francisco. Notes from lovers... Deep material. Loving, yearning. Pornographic at times. Pornographic a lot of times! Then I discover a thick manila envelope. 'Joyous Things' I wrote with black Sharpie marker across it twenty-something years ago... the passionate correspondence from my summer with Joy... a Thai woman from Brooklyn who rocked my world. We met through a mutual friend... my beach buddy, Kim. She tagged along one day and it was instant sparks. She'd jump on the train to Long Island so we could sun at Robert Moses State Park beach on the south shore of Long Island. We'd walk to the nude beach and tan all day with the pervs under fluttering dragon kites. The time we had together was one of the most intense I've ever experienced. We compacted a lifetime of sex and romance into a few months. We pleased each other to such a high level it was nearly impossible to come down. We turned each other into an aphrodisiac, which became addictive. Her memory still lingers with me... the things we did, even her smile. But as fast as she came into my life, she was gone...

ghosted me. With trepidation I crack her first letter, which still lingers with the scent of her fragrance... Spiritual Sky Opium. Her letters are intricately designed... even the envelopes with hand-drawn geometric borders are done with loving care. I slide one out of the envelope. An envelope marked in pen with an exotic cat before a sly-looking sun.

She talks about receiving my mix tape... I remember it... started with "Give Me Your Love" from Superfly. Curtis Mayfield. "I'm walking around Park Slope with a GIANT grin. I love this mix tape! Each song makes my heart sing" followed by three hearts. "How'd you get so sweet, lover? You have no idea how surprised I am to share this time with you. I want to smother you with kisses..."

I close it quickly because my heart jumps and I trip back in time to a lush bed with marshmallow pillows and afternoon delights.

But I'm too intrigued to stop now. I continue through the pile. I pick the second letter... a red crimson spot in hand-brushed watercolor wash, like the Japanese flag. I can't tell if the paper is aged or was always a soft parchment. I slide out the note. Each page is a crimson swirl on white with beautiful black pen lettering. Sharp letters, almost foreign in their design.

Darlin',

Missing you here in bed as the rain falls outside. I had a lonely dinner in front of the tele. Looking at my naked reflection in the brass doorknob between these written lines. The softness of your lips warms my soul, when you kiss me...

It continues on to places I can't share. The papers are slightly smeared from the paint. Remnants of her fingerprints are smudged around. Her passionate words linger in my head and body. But as I filter down over the stack of love letters, the beautiful intricate envelopes and papers become less and less adorned. The painstaking work of glued magazine images, patch-worked together in exotic murals and interesting stickers swirled together with paints and pen cartouches give way to more bleak and business-like envelopes. Even a dried flower, lovingly pressed to a black sheet and adorned in gold paint, crumbles in my hand. The letters are passionate, yet casted in self-doubt about her worth to me... thoughts of her not being good enough, thoughts of her being interesting enough and the creeping of fears. Her not wanting to say 'I Love You' because they're big words. Scared of the possibilities. The battle waging in her heart. Scared to make mistakes. Fears of me saying 'I Love You' to *her*. "Because behind my happy, fun, silly exterior I am filled with doubt and darkness."

It's hard to distinguish if she's truly at odds with herself, with her emotions.... or letting me off easy while still enjoying our time together. Perhaps both. It seems like the laying of groundwork to let me off in the future under the guise of me being too good for her, or she not being good enough for me. A gentle "It's not you it's me." The letter has a brickwork pattern on the top and bottom. A stone walkway... maybe walking mentally out of the picture. "How much do you really want to know me?" says one. The statement of someone with skeletons in their closet. I reach the end of the stack. The last note. A plain white envelope. So plain it's almost cold to the touch. And the letter inside... a computer printed note. Done with an antiquated 'tech' font... OCR-A maybe... the green computer font you see in the movies as the camera is swooping over a Middle Eastern country at night, introducing Seal Team 6 and their mission. This is done in a smudgy charcoal grey on milky watermarked paper of a bygone era. There's no style. Barely a hint of punctuation. Not even an indent to separate paragraphs. A block of letters. But the message is clear before it's even read. She went into icy computer mode. The Terminator of relationships... "How do I begin my response, my defense?" she states. Obviously, a return volley from an impassioned letter from me. One of many in a chain that probably increased in emotional depth till it overloaded everything we'd built. "I can't list specifically the reasons it (the relationship) just isn't for me, without hurting your feelings."... "I'm sorry for making such a clean break," she says. "Please know I thoroughly enjoyed the time we did spend together... But A.J. I knew from the beginning that it was really only a temporary situation."

  Well, at least *she* knew... and it goes on. Some of it cutting and some of it backhanded compliments. The nature of it seems that I misinterpreted everything... and that has happened before... to me, and a billion other people as well I'm sure, but reading our past correspondence it's clear... we were connecting on a deep level. Her letters are proof I wasn't dreaming things... But perhaps that's the way love is... or perhaps that's the way LUST is. "I hope you find someone worthy of all your little treasures. Be well. Joy."

  Lastly, a photograph of her. One I took. It's at the Cloisters garden in Washington Heights on the Upper West Side of Manhattan. It's black and white... sepia-tone really.

She's smiling, squinting from the sun. But her bright smile is forced. I probably noticed then but pretended not to. The relationship is already over. You can see it in her eyes.

I heard later from Kim, the friend that introduced us, that she was married soon after... on Halloween. To the boyfriend she was with the whole time. Thumbing through the letters, she never gave me her last name... I don't remember it. I didn't ask. This was not an accidental omission on her part. Maybe I got caught in the lust and mistook it for love. I don't know. All I know is that she got into me deep and I've never forgotten her in all my years. And I never will. Reading the letters again I'm transported once more... to those times... to her arms. Into her body.

But the past is the past and I throw the entire correspondence into the trash with the endless piles of Mr. Christmas tabletop sketches, some design concepts for Craftsman tools tree ornaments, packaging art for a Xena: Warrior Princess 12-inch action figure and the ghost of the splintered Mickey Mouse roller coaster.

BUGGIN' OUT

9

MICROWAVES AND DIAMOND RINGS

"We're getting rid of the microwave because we don't need it."

That's the announcement I get from my wife as I enter the kitchen on a clear afternoon on September 24. Not "hello, dear, how was your day?" Not "You're the best!" I don't even have time to ask about her day... her *birth*day. I'm not expecting her to spin around and present me with a freshly baked apple pie... apron tied tightly around her waist. But I'm certainly not expecting this info bomb. Somewhere she heard microwaves are dangerous and now ours is dangerous.

Our close friends don't have one! When someone mentions to them "I don't see a microwave in your kitchen," they act as if they're boxes made from weapons-grade plutonium. I've had a microwave for 35 plus years. I consider it an essential kitchen item. Indispensable even. It heats everything from gravy to popcorn in milliseconds.

But apparently, we're European now... two-hour

lunches, siestas and closing up shop in the middle of the day to the detriment of businesses all over the area... that type of thing. Like the time I went to Paris and the entire city closed down for lunch and I couldn't find a pen. I spent two hours hunting for a pen to write something down and couldn't because the entire city was shuttered. Unfortunately, whatever thought I had to write down was lost forever and won't appear in this book.

In conclusion, reheating a bowl of rice in milliseconds will now give way to a metal pot to heat it on the stove, which requires gas for the burner, the pot will need to be washed with water and effort to do the job—soap water gets into the environment and pollutes our drinking water. What appears to be a better way of life is actually killing the environment and wasting more time than it appears. Anti-microwave sentiment is actually killing our environment. And even worse, it's robbing us of our precious time. It's not a decision to be taken lightly... it's our livelihood at stake. Sure, it takes a few minutes longer to heat things, but it quantifies as time passes... in years we'll have wasted countless hours heating rice when we could have been writing or creating art, or zipping through a season of *The Bachelor*. This is her idea and I'll stand by it... this is a woman who shops at Costco hungry. Food-Stuffs she would of thought was garbage six hours earlier is suddenly the world's greatest invention... "yogurt tubes! Amazing. Let's get this crate of 824 yogurt tubes."

Only hours before this dreadful announcement, I was at the jewelers. Two checks had cleared, one from my job and one from a freelance gig I'd done a few months prior, and I confidently transferred money from savings into checking and nervously pulled the trigger on the final ring payment... the last chunk of money on the expensive rock set in shiny platinum. To a caveman, completely worthless because it's inedible. To the modern man, some representation of wealth and prestige. A status symbol. To a modern woman, a cat's toy that flips the eyes into gleaming saucers. But to the practical man, a worthless tool when the zombie apocalypse spreads through his sleepy little town.

The jeweler asks me when I plan to give it to my wife and I tell him for our anniversary in November, which is a solid two months away, so he suggests I keep it in a safe place. "Not on the car seat" chimes his sister from the back. I joke that I plan to toss it in a paint can in my workshop and we chuckle way too hard over the absurdity. I assure him that I'm going to keep it in the large safe at my parent's house, which is a load of shit. I actually *do* stuff the ring into an old paint can and plunk it down on the workbench of my workshop amongst the other drippy paint cans. It's a perfect cover because the workshop is a dank cesspool. I don't want to tell my parents about the ring because they'll panic and tell me how expensive it is even though I just bought the thing and I know how expensive it is.

But my parents have always equated the value of life with how things cost, and not by what is actually valuable... time. In my life, in accordance with my parents, you simply don't talk about money. Let me rephrase that statement... they constantly talk about money; they don't talk about *spending* money. It's met with a sudden bombastic, hyperbolic sense of anxiety. My parents have been saving for retirement since the moment they opened a bank account and it's driven them mad with a scrambling sense of savings panic. It will *never* be enough and it's impossible to be comfortable, knowing that retirement will come.

Telling my parents you went out for a burger is to tell them you bought a vintage Porsche.

"Burgers? That's kind of expensive!"

Then it continues with eyebrow-raising inquiries as to *where* you got burgers...

"Really? Where'd you go?"

If you tell them, it may be met with severe disappointment, like when I failed sociology in college.

"Meehan's? That place is kind of expensive, yea?"

And then before you know it, you're justifying sirloin over ground chuck. So it's best not to tell them about the ring... or burgers... or anything. My wife and I have gotten to the point where we simply pretend we don't do anything.

"What'd you do this weekend?" they ask.

"Us? Stared at the wall..."

Of course, having a child who gives up the goods is problematic. Fortunately, he's exactly like I was as a kid... has the worst freakin' memory... can't remember what you told him five minutes ago. Although he'll drop a bomb on Christmas morning at my parent's house and spill an itemized list of everything I got my wife in descending price order.

I will give my parents credit though. At least they have a retirement plan. My retirement plan involves a car, and me driving over a cliff in a tragic accident for the life insurance money.

But the ring's been paid for and I have a level of comfort in the fact that the deed is done. It's difficult to drop many thousands of dollars on a shiny rock... it feels wrong, but it's what she wants and I'm willing to do it. The fingers need shiny rocks on them... that's just the way life works. We're sophisticated creatures. It's what separates us from animals. We shit in fresh water, have a box in our kitchen that keeps our dead meat cold, we prance around on spiky shoes and wear polished rocks on our arm sticks.

•••

My wife's September birthday is the beginning of the holiday crunch countdown. Time is flying by. In mid-January we'll be talking about how it was just Christmas and how fast the year is going.

"I'm still writing last year's date on my checks!"

Then the kids will be going back to school at the end of summer...

"The summer just flew by! I can't believe it."

Then we'll be talking about the holidays again...

"Christmas? Oh, God! Don't get me started! I can't even! It was just Summer!!"

The eternal rush. Back-to-school ads at the beginning of Summer. Christmas in September. We never enjoy the moment. It's not possible. We celebrate Rita's birthday with take-out food on the beach... shrimp korma and chicken fingers. On the way, my son is already talking about Christmas, which is three months away. I clutch my purse strings. My money is already being spent and it gives me jitters. I can feel the ghost of Christmas future... it's called the January credit card bill. I just gave my wife a cheap greeting card filled with expensive cash for her birthday. My son drew balloons on a folded piece of copy paper. He got out of the deal easy. I've got jewelry to expense and their favorite holiday is breathing frosty air down the back of my neck. Max insists on eggs and bacon on Christmas morning. At least I can check something off the endless holiday list... the Christmas breakfast menu is set. A load off my mind.

Our ten-year anniversary drops the day before Thanksgiving. I pull the ring from the paint can and it shines like a crazy diamond. Because it is a diamond. Didn't get stolen. A paint can is better than a safe! Rita and I go out to dinner at Honu, a fancy restaurant where we are tucked cozily next to a fireplace, as I requested. We talk about everything that has led up to that moment... the tree, the wish, the hieroglyphics in the little notebook... the ups and downs... the health issues and our amazing son.

Ten years before, when I gave her a simple silver engagement ring over plates of hamburgers at Flea Market, a French Brasserie in the East Village of Manhattan, Rita couldn't have been more confused. We were living together and having a baby, so we were married in spirit already. So when I proposed, she thought I was giving her a random gift. We laugh about that now.

A decade later, I present her with a diamond in platinum. She loves it. Of course she does. It's a pretty big diamond! I've nearly gone broke paying for it. Rita grew up on beans and rice, which is good because we'll be eating a lot of it for the next few years.

We try and enjoy our anniversary, but in reality it's DECEMBER. The holidays are here. They've *been* here... which means Christmas. The other holidays have been obliterated. It starts the mili-second Halloween ends... *before* Halloween ends. Wander the aisles of your local everything-mart and the plastic jack-o-lanterns are on sale. 50% off. The holly is snaking in. It's snuck in. It's here! Fuck Thanksgiving! Thanksgiving is a zone you need to tolerate before the blinking lights go up. Two months of Ho Ho Ho and All I Want For Christmas Is You. Don't get me started on Hanukkah and Kwanza and the others. You know the deal... and my birthday is tossed in there somewhere too... lost in time. Don't get me wrong, I love Christmas. Lots of people do. But it starts at the end of summer. It's out of control. I see red bows and jewelry ads while my nose is still sunburned.

I see a picture on Facebook or some other social manipulator... an African girl. Standing in a garbage dump. Holding an IV attached to what I assume is her mother, who is lying on the ground, rail-thin, eyes shut. Mom is dying. God knows of what... AIDS, Ebola. She stares off into the distance. Her look says it all. "What am I going to do?" It almost seems like too much. I realize there's poor sanitation and people are dying. But why are they dying in the middle of a garbage dump? Can they move a few 100 yards out of the dump? Or is the entire country a dump? It's an image that stings. Manipulated for impact or not, I don't know. I don't know what I'm seeing anymore. My eyes see but my mind doubts and my heart is stuck in the middle.

The December holidays can be the most wonderful

time of the year. Good food, good friends and tons of powerful drinks with heavy creams and warm spiced wines. The holidays can also be a source of sadness for some, but there's always a glimmer of hope for the unemployed, the sick and the downtrodden even at this time of year. They say that it's better to give than to receive, and that's true. But our giving muscles should be working at full-strength during the whole year and not just in the middle chunk of December. Sliding a few bucks out of your wallet to help the less fortunate seems like a stunning act of kindness, but it's more a selfish act to warm the cockles of your own heart rather than helping others. Try giving in May after you've gotten your tax return instead of getting that obnoxious 75" HD plasma television you've been eyeballing.

As a child at Christmas, I was spoiled rotten by my grandparents and all my parents' siblings. I received an absurd amount of gifts. You would have thought I'd grow up to be a spoiled adult who expected everything to be given to me, but now that I'm older I couldn't care less about receiving holiday gifts. In fact, I don't want anything at all. There's nothing that I want or really need -- and if I do need it, I can buy it on my own. I've actually become more of a minimalist and enjoy the freedom (both mentally and physically) of owning very little. I feel comforted to know that at any temperamental moment, I can throw it all by the wayside and go backpacking around the planet a few dozen times... if the desire should arise.

One of the great horrors of the holidays is receiving a gift that you don't want or like. Not only do you have to strain your acting chops pretending to like it, you get depressed later on because you realize someone actually paid hard-earned money on something that you'll toss in your closet and not see again until you do a spring cleaning or move. I'm all-in on the capitalist ideals of the USA, but wasting money on dopey items is heartbreaking no matter how you slice it. I'm not talking about so-called "bad" gifts like socks or even sweaters with doe-eyed kittens on them. Those tend to be useful once you reach a certain age. I'm talking about mind-benders like grandfather clocks made of cheese or a 50-inch turquoise felt sun-hat that Goldie Hawn sported in a magazine back in 1981. Even something as thoughtful as a man's wallet can be wince-inducing if it's red leather with giant white stitching. This is probably why the gift certificate is so popular these days. People realize taste is a personal thing and pink jumpsuits should be left to certain sections of our population, and not staring up from the lap of your nephew on Christmas morning... Unless he asked for a pink jumpsuit.

The absolute worst gifts to receive are those regifted. The dreadful holiday regift is doubly horrifying because it's blatantly obvious that the gift was shifted from one party to the next. It's embarrassing to receive because you were either forgotten about in the first place or given something no one wanted. It's possible the regift you receive has been regifted four or five time. If little Johnny gets a box of chocolate-covered prunes, you know something went terribly wrong down the chain. It gets to the point where people can't remember what's in the wrapping anymore and handing off a regift could be a game of Russian Roulette. "Oh look, you gave our six year-old a set of fireplace matches; something she's always wanted."

One year when I was 18, my parents' friends gifted me

a box of pumpkin candy. I took it with a smile as I'm not one to turn down a free gift—I came to their house with nothing and left with something. But what was so ham-handed about this gift was it was in Thanksgiving-like packaging. Not only was it regifted, it was regifted from a different holiday. Halloween candy would have been preferential to Thanksgiving pumpkin candy. I like pumpkin, but from October 1st through the end of November, everything that's made into food is made with pumpkin and I feel candy is one thing that should be exempt. To add insult to injury, the pumpkin candy box looked as though it'd been stomped by a pack of wild boars. The cellophane wrapping was tearing in multiple spots and each box corner was at certain levels of crushed. At that point it should have been tossed in the garbage. Basically, I was the garbage man in this one-sided gift exchange. "We were going to toss this in the trash, but we gave it to you instead." Hey, you know the saying... I was once disappointed that I had no hat until I met a man with no head. Take what you get and make the best of it.

    But sometimes no gift is just as good, and sometimes better, than a poorly decided regift. My friend Chip once got a wooden cane as a gift. He was a healthy and vigorous fifteen year-old, but his uncle thought a beat-up wooden cane would be something he would appreciate. Two days later, Chip whittled the thing into a lethal weapon that was used to stab a punching bag till it bled sand, so perhaps his uncle was correct. But it's best to err on the side of caution. When someone walks into your house, hand them a cookie or a stiff cocktail. They'll forget about gift exchanging in no time.

•••

It's the very beginning of January 2020, Just after a celebration I dislike... New Year's Eve. I don't really like going around telling everyone to have a Happy New Year until we've properly mourned the death of the old year. I've never felt particularly great when December 31st rolls around. I usually feel static and depressed—a bit muddy, I suppose. While most people have glitter-laden cardboard hats glued to their hair, prancing about in black-tie attire and sipping cheap champagne, I prefer to sit quietly at home and decompress.

The year worked very hard to give us the ups and downs that we enjoy reviewing at year's end. We make lists on the best of everything that happened during the course of the year—the best books, movies and television shows—these things will be neatly wrangled into a grouping and laid out for our light reading pleasure. Lists of restaurants, influential people, trends and whatever someone can conjure into a top-ten list. People like tight packages with things buttoned up for their ease of use and a top-ten list is pretty easy to swallow. Sometimes these lists start at the beginning of December, propelling us to exclaim, "Hey, there's 1/12th of the year left!" Especially since December is when filmmakers flood the market with their Oscar-bait releases. It seems premature to make a list of the year's events before December 31. But that's just me. Time magazine releases their person of the year in early December, but unless someone came along at the tail end and cured cancer, I guess that one was pretty much wrapped up.

My wife and I are standing in line at Zara, a giant

clothing store, exchanging Christmas gifts she got a few weeks ago. There are 25 people on line. All have about five to seven articles of clothing. The process of checking out feels like an eternity. There are two cashiers. When a customer steps up, the cashier takes each article of clothing and scans it, shakes it, gently folds it, carefully places it down and punches what seems like 50 numbers into the monitor. The customer has coupons and a return... it fucking takes *forever*! I feel my life passing by... wasting away. It's painful. I'm a big fan of Apple computers. I think Steve Jobs was a genius. Total dick, but a genius. You can walk into an Apple store and buy a $12,000 computer in about three minutes and be out the door. Have these companies learned nothing from the Apple process? No need for lines. Check out is seamless and easy. It's the wave of the future. I'm on line at Zara for 25 minutes. It's ridiculous. You'd have thought they were giving away clothes, but this a line to actually *pay* for clothing. My wife hates my impatience, but I point out to her that my life is trickling away. You know what you can do in 25 minutes? Change the world! And it's not just these 25 minutes. It's all the 25 minutes of all the waiting lines combined. I can't be alone in this thought. We're given the gift of life, yet I am spending it staring blankly at the wall for 25 minutes, waiting to buy an overpriced shirt made by the small hands of slave children from a country we're currently bombing.

  This is when I truly feel the weight of mortality. Death, in the end, will be one fell swoop. BAM! Over quickly... hopefully, if you're lucky, and not a long-suffering painful death like cancer or being crushed in half by a piano on the sidewalk. But death can also come in little chunk -- in small scoops from your soul -- in tiny doses throughout the day. Like smoking a cigarette or standing in line at Zara.

We get home from exchanging the gifts. It's been a degrading and tortuous affair. I flop onto the couch and flip on the a Knicks basketball game. After a tax commercial, I'm presented with a woman so elated, you'd have thought she'd been crowned queen of the Earth. She spins and faces us as her obnoxious husband wraps a *huge* diamond necklace around her outstretched neck. It's almost Valentine's Day. Time to show your love by spending your life savings on a strand of polished rocks. It takes all my energy to keep from throwing the remote through our 75" HD TV.

BUGGIN' OUT

10

FOOD, GLORIOUS FOOD!

I've had food poisoning about eight times in my life. This isn't a boast, it's just fact. My parents love telling people I barely ate anything as a child.

"The only vegetable he ate was lettuce. No dressing!"

They'd shake their heads at the incredulous nature of it all. Similar shock abounds when someone states their grandpa ate the *entire* apple. "Seeds and everything!" they claim, as silverware skates across plates in a clatter. The news of me eating nothing as a kid comes as a shock to my wife as she's seen me eat just about anything with life coursing through its veins... animals and leafy greens alike. She watches survival shows where the contestants eat alligator testicles and she asks if I'd eat that.

"With the proper sauce, sure."

I've contemplated everything from bugs to the parts of animals most people consider to be the basis of glue or dried into powder and fed to other less conscious animals. As a parlor game she'll toss out a random animal and its body part and ask if I'll eat it... like the Mad Libs of vittles.

"Would you eat a <u>Boiled Donkey's Penis</u> on a bed of lettuce?"

My wife is one to talk as she's the one who got me hooked on grilled chicken hearts, my favorite Brazilian delicacy. Perhaps it's not hard to see why I got food poisoning eight times. The first time was from a BLT on white toast, which you won't find roaming the debilitating desert plains of South Africa on *Naked and Afraid*. But you'll find one at the corner deli. A smear of room temperature mayo slathered on greasy undercooked bacon will send you chucking into the toilet on the half-hour like clockwork.

As a kid, my sister got ill on Burger King and vowed never to eat it again, which is a promise I believe she's kept. Dogs will eat their own vomit five minutes after chucking it up. They do a quick circle and discover it as a completely new food source. I don't have a memory that terrible, but I can feel ill from say, a dense chicken pot pie, vow never to look at one ever again, then three days later say:

"you know what I'm in the mood for? Chicken pot pie."

The second time I got food poisoning was in 1982 when I was about 11. I ate a two-pound lobster at one of our family favorites called Glynn's, a place so out of business, it became a Mexican restaurant, then leveled to dirt and reconstructed into a bank. So, complaining now is out of the question. But I hurled into the dawn's early light and vowed never to eat lobster again.

The third time I got food poisoning was on lobster. This was at a restaurant in Huntington called The Harbor Inn. It was one of my favorite places because, when I was 10, I had the pleasure of meeting my favorite football player, defensive end Mark Gastineau, a one-man wrecking crew for the New York Jets. My father got me in the door of a Lions Club meeting so I could stare at the back of Mark's head. He signed a piece of paper for me and it was a "I'll never wash this cheek again" moment, similar to *The Brady Bunch* when Marcia was kissed on the cheek by Davy Jones and refused to wash her face. But my bout with food poisoning came a few years later. A steaming lobster was presented to me, and to my horror, was filled with orange sludge. My uncle assured me I was lucky because it was filled with glorious roe! I saw sea slime. Not yet old enough to appreciate the beauty of roe, or sushi, or anything of that nature, I washed the succulent chunks of meat free of roe in lemon butter and gorged on the sea bug with delight. Night in the bathroom.

Shocking as it may seem, but the fourth time I got food poisoning was on lobster. You'd think I'd quit eating lobster, but I really like lobster. Especially after I grew older and discovered the glorious lobster roll, which, if you are not privy, is when they take an entire lobster, deshell it, chop it up with a touch of mayo, butter and herbs, and serve it on a toasted hot dog bun. Pure heaven. Unfortunately, this langosta trifecta happened on a weekend getaway with my girlfriend Teri who'd booked a tryst at a bed and breakfast in Kennebunkport, Maine. I remember going out for the day, enjoyed a walk along some twisted seaside rocks, then dinner at a chic captain's den where fish tanks were inset the royal blue walls and ropes thick enough to hold cruise ships in place hung like garland. Before dinner was over, my lips began to tingle and soon I was melted across the bed of our quaint b and b, retching into a wastebasket until Teri dragged me like a cavewoman into her Jeep for the ride home. Perhaps one might think I'm allergic to the clawed crustacean, but having eaten yards upon glorious yards of them, that fails to prove true.

My buddy Ned once got food poisoning in Shri Lanka. He was backpacking with friends across the south Asian Pacific. On a warm beachside restaurant, the waiter presented him a fish whose eyes had ghosted over in cataracts. He was on the fence about it, knew he should say no, but so as not to insult the restaurant he had them prepare it and brought to the table. Bad idea. He said he was so ill he could barely move. His friends had to drag him out of bed, toss on his backpack and push him through the jungle to his next destination, which hopefully had fresher fish on the menu.

By the time the sun hit my room at 14, I was in full food experimenting mode. I'd eaten beef tongue and was a huge fan of calf's liver. Venison was on the menu as was duck, game birds, rabbit, frogs' legs and anything yanked from the sea. I'd tasted snake, boar and many of the critters you can shoot scampering in the woods. In the mid-teen years, the boy's body becomes essentially a garbage disposal. Frozen dinners were a staple. My parents went out a lot and left me to fend for myself. Salisbury steak was a buzzword in our house. Kids today have Netflix and Chill, but I had Hungry Man and *Love Boat*. When I reached 16, I would go to the supermarket and buy a pound of a bacon substitute called Sizzlean, fry it up and eat the entire thing myself. This wonderful amalgamation was salted ground pork refashioned into a strip of bacon. How it fared better than actual bacon, I can't say. The package claimed a 50% reduction in fat from normal bacon, but having prepared it in oil slicks of its own lard, that was probably false advertising. How's my cholesterol, you wonder? I had it checked in early 2005 and it's fine.

I've always been thin with a circus act ability to gorge on food and never gain weight.

"How many Scotch Eggs will A.J. eat at the BBQ tonight? Four? Five?"

The sixth time I got food poisoning may actually have been basic over-eating. Piggybacking on four stiff margaritas, I consumed a huge platter of half-priced sushi, the kind *flowered* around a round plastic tray and passed at cocktail parties. When that failed to satisfy, I topped it off with a Big Mac. Now that I think about it, probably overindulgence. By the way, not a good combo. I've made some unusual food parings before... Sushi and breakfast sausage links, Ketchup over tuna salad and double espressos, Ice cream eaten with Doritos, and smoothies consisting of any kind of refrigerator leftover.

In the mid-80s, my Uncle Paul went to a Mets game and ate nine hot dogs. One for every inning. He didn't hurl, but he had to put a mortgage on his home to pay for them. Sporting events are great for food. Most stadiums have raised the bar to gourmet-level with the food. A few Summer's ago, I was gifted tickets to the Hyundai club at CitiField, a private area reserved for high-paying folks who prefer shaved roast beef paired with tarragon-roasted potatoes over a dirty water hot dog. Still, I went for the hotdogs. Bacon wrapped deep-fried hot dogs to be precise. I ate five of them. After the girl who served them to me lowered her eyebrows, she watched me dance them over to the nacho area and cover them in warm neon cheese. Then I got on the dinner line and, bypassing the roast beef, asked the chef to glaze my gooey dogs with caramelized onions. Let me tell you there were some jealous eyes on me that night. Fat, jealous eyes.

The seventh case, and I should say, worst case of food poisoning I ever got was on a slice of pizza. It was 2002 and I'd been released from my toy design job early on a gorgeous summer evening and nuzzled into a warm slice from my favorite place on St. Mark's Place in New York City's East Village. The slice and I were in perfect harmony on my 9th street stoop, when my stomach tried to spasm out, what felt like a hot coal sitting in my gut. It was vicious. How a reaction could happen so fast I couldn't say. Was the mozzarella left on the counter all night? Perhaps the sauce fermented next to the water heater, or the dough neglected in some terrible way. All I can say is I probably should have been hospitalized. But I fought all night, vomiting violently into my apartment toilet till I was twisted like a dish rag. Lying on the cool tile floor, my ear to the air vent, I heard the upstairs neighbor tell his wife, "The poor bastard downstairs has been throwing up all night long. I think he almost died."

On a gorgeous summer evening in 2017, my wife, son and I got takeout hamburgers and brought them to a local beach where we set up dinner on a picnic table. In a flash, a freak windstorm blew through our dinner like a hurricane. Out of nowhere, 50-mile-an-hour winds blasted our food off the table and into oblivion... napkins, dots in the sky... food, plastered in the sand... everything, obliterated into the ether... and as fast as it came, the wind storm left... a 2 minute flash wind from the heavens... environmental FU. We were dumfounded. Good food, gone missing. There's was nothing to clean up. It turned to dust. We chalked it up as a sign... the gods preventing food poisoning, and that's just how I accepted it. Thanked the heavens and moved on. This type of thing shouldn't happen to nice people, but obviously does. We limped home and had Tupperware tapas and leftover ice cream cake.

My final food poisoning excursion (as of this printing) was on a hamburger. No windstorms blew in to stop this one. That occurred a few years ago... the night before a ski trip... right after the Christmas crunch. At our local diner, the waitress apologized multiple times for my order taking so long because the short-order cook called in sick, which should have been the first clue to run. A bunch of burgers and fries, how hard can it be? Figured, easy clean-up, easy to get away the next day. I was wrong. Who they got to take that chef's place was not clear, perhaps the dishwasher, or the guy who clobbers the rats with a broom, but my 'medium rare' burger was more like 'just murdered' and I ate it anyway even though the little man on my shoulder kept saying "That looks pretty rare, dumbass." The fries were like wet napkins and I was convinced nothing had been cooked over the temperature of 70 degrees. I awoke in the middle of the night about 5 hours after eating and visited the bathroom, a place familiar to me in so many ways. The cool white tiles, the humming fan, the obnoxious bright light. I prayed to the porcelain goddess a bit, but in terms of foulness, it was a solid 7 out of 10. I still had the usual effects of upchucking... the sweating, the runny nose and the occasional shouting of "oh god" to no one in particular.

    I was picked up bright and early the next morning by friends and driven to the mountain. My family stuck me on a pair of skis and pushed me down a mountain to my next destination, hoping that the next place had better burgers. Or at least, properly cooked ones.

11

GENERATION X, Y AND Z

My son and I are in the kitchen having breakfast. Black coffee for me, some kind of mouth-cutting chocolate puffs cereal for him... bird seeds for our cockatiel, Zen. Max is 9, but asks for some coffee and I oblige with a few splashes into a cup that I mix with sugar. He hums with delight and a coffee addiction is born. A few years ago, my wife and son went to Brazil for a month to visit Vivian, her sister, and Vinicios, Max's cousin. After three weeks I came to join them and found that Max had been drinking large glasses of coffee every morning. Needless to say, I wasn't pleased. Beer, not a problem. Coffee... no way. I was positive had I arrived a week later, Max would have been smoking six-inch brown cigarettes and finishing every statement with the word *Fin*.

And now, he has the coffee vibe awoken in his blood again, raised from the dead like a caffeinated Leviathan. Soon he'll be begging for fresh ground dark roast prior to his 4th grade grind and my morning routine will be an unwieldy three-hour circus act.

    We talk about his childhood in comparison to mine. He's a highly intelligent kid... supremely aware of how his life is going. Understands already that life for him is very different compared to mine at his age. He knows that Rita and I, like every other parent in the USA, are varying degrees of helicopter parenting, who were spoon-fed a healthy dose of 11 o-clock news terror and sky-is-falling mentality. He knows when I was a kid, I had more freedom... didn't have to wear a bike helmet, wandered the streets by myself and munched on handfuls of lead-laced paint chips. He's incredibly perceptive... although my son forgot his last name the other day when we opened a bank account for him, so I'm not sure where the high intelligence ends, and the raw stupidity begins. But he's right. Life was different for me. I wandered the streets, jumped the fence and trekked to the next neighborhood to hang with my friend Brad Hennegan, my small friend with a big smile. We'd spend the entire day together and I'd return at night for dinner. I'd thrash the 'hood on my bike, without a helmet, or knee pads, or any kind of first aid kit... whip through razor-sharp tree branches and hop over hypodermic needles on jumps made from plyboard found on a neighbors' asbestos garbage pile at the end of their lava driveway. I drank lead-laced water from a rusty garden hose and rarely wore sunscreen.

    How he got that perception about me I don't know. Perhaps he's been listening to the yarns I've spun at the dinner table after a few beers. Tales that have gotten him laughing and sometimes crying on the floor. Like the time my friend Andy and I stole all the neighbors' metal garbage can lids to use as knight shields and dumped them in my bedroom closet... my father discovering them and hitting the roof. He still talks about that.

My son's realization that he is working with a new set of criteria is an amazing relief for me in a few ways. First, it cuts some of the edge off the fact that I *know* I'm not giving him the life I was having which was a really wonderful childhood that felt very free, and he accepts that. Two, it helps me to get over that nagging pain in my soul that I'm not a good-enough parent... a feeling every good parent has deep inside of them... that they are not doing enough, helping enough... not spending enough time with them, even though we are literally doing *everything* in the world for them. And three, it helps me to know that he is prepared to move forward in this life as the parents we (and everyone else is in the world) are, and that he's working with the precedent that's been set, a foundation we've laid, the laws and rules we've created, and the tools he has to work with. But he's also hearing from his teachers who are about my age, and how their lives were similar to mine. Freedom to explore... life before cell phones, before the internet and before video games with graphics so real, you're inside virtual reality. You know... caveman life.

When my father was about six, he and his younger brother Greg bum-rushed my grandmother and stuffed her into the bedroom closet and locked it. They shook cereal boxes and created complicated trails on the floor... mimicking the cartoons on TV when they would lay twisty lines of black powder across the desert so as to be at a safe distance when the powder was lit and the trail flashed towards an absurd pile of TNT kegs that would replicate an atom bomb. My grandfather returned from his city job to find the boys eating candy on the couch, the house a mess and the cooking pots cold... my grandmother still locked in the closet... a mere eight hours since she was tossed in. Once released, she flew into a rage and whipped the boys on their rear-ends so they couldn't sit for days. This was back before the cavemen... probably in the dinosaur era. Long before... anything fun, really. Kids played with sticks and a toy was made of wood.

Tucked inside a Currier and Ives-style book of large prints showing various waterfowl landing on cattail-lined ponds, I flip through and discover a large 14" x 11" black and white photo of me at three years old. I'm cutting a big white frosted birthday cake that says *Happy Birthday A.J.* My hair is white. A towhead with hand-me-down checkered overalls and a white turtleneck. This is set off by my mother and the patchy couch in the background and the lace tablecloth... the patterns swirl in psychedelia. My mother, flared-out in a flower-patterned blouse fit for drapes, is guiding my hand with a long cream-covered knife. My chubby cousin Mary-Lin, in horizontal stripes, licks her chops in the background.

It's about as far back as I can go with my memory. I don't remember being born that's for sure... pretty sure I don't remember being one... or even two... but I remember that three-year old. Just like my son said, that kid was free in the 70s, long before the modern daily news stream updates of serial killers and rapists.

One day, I wandered to a different neighborhood, roamed the streets looking for a buddy to play with. Upon returning, my mother was incensed... where had I been? When I couldn't find a playmate I went hunting for my sister, who I located at a friend's playing with dolls. They kicked me out. I was annoying them, so I steamed and stomped home alone... stubbed my toe on the curb and cried as I got to my mother.

She was so relieved to see me. She'd already lost me once... the previous year of 1975 when I stumbled into the back yard wearing my auburn fall clothing, plopped into a pile of unbagged leaves and napped. Upon wakening a few hours later, I discovered the entire emergency broadcast system in our yard. A cluster of police and firemen comforting my mother as I yawned into view.

My cousin Mary-Lin lived down the street. She was miserable. Her father was an abusive alcoholic and a madman. He was addicted to calling random women on the phone and saying obscene things to them. Eventually the police caught up to him and threw him in jail. She ate to offset the crazy, and her mother Patsy went into a state of paranoia. They bolted out of town not soon after to start a new life and we weren't far behind. We lived in the middle of nowhere... Coram, Long Island... in a starter home that started to hold us back. It was a bare box with one wiry tree. One day my mother went to plant some flowers and discovered the house builder used our yard to illegally dump. Our soil was a mixture of pummeled concrete and old clothing rags. Not ideal for fresh veggies. Our neighbor was a humorless, grim-faced Jehovah's Witness who would stand in his yard with his arms folded in anger, burning a death-stare at anyone that crossed his view. One evening, he came to our door with a flock of Witnesses, demanding we house them for a week. Imagine anyone's shock when my father refused. Our neighbor's attitude darkened from charcoal-grey to a black that is difficult to find on a Pantone color book.

Fortunately, we were able to escape Coram in 1977 and move to Huntington about 45 minutes west. Coram was a dump and still is unfortunately kind of a dump... no offense to the people who live in Coram... all fine people, I'm sure. But now that I'm back on Long Island and watch the local news, Coram grabs headlines nightly with a shooting or gas station robbery. Growing up, I thought Long Island was kind of boring... a thought most people probably have about their stymied little town. Having left for a while and returned, I realize that Long Island is absolutely bonkers, bat-shit crazy. It's like its own biosphere – a savage island connected to the rest of the United States by giant metal cables. It has its own accent! My mother would call me in Manhattan and complain about the people interviewed on the news as I held the receiver a foot from my ear,

"Oh my gaawd! I can't bu-leeve the pee-pul on da neewz with their lawn-guy-land accents."

I didn't have the heart to tell her.

"yea, ma. Unbelievable."

I was lucky in my timing getting into the world. Born in what Hunter S. Thompson deemed the foul year of our Lord, 1971. I was the child of two influential decades: the 70s and 80s... Instantly identifiable through clothing, pop culture, music and Halloween costumes. My parents were 23 and 24 years old when I was born. My sister arrived five years before. They focused their parenting paranoia on her and by the time I was ten, I was flying under the radar. Free to be me. The early 80s came around and it was perfectly acceptable to ask how much cocaine you should bring to the party.

I wasn't just a latchkey kid... I had a latchkey life.

My parents weren't negligent. It's just the way it was. They worked. My mother had multiple jobs. My father was gone all day building an architecture business. We let ourselves into the house and took care of ourselves. My parents took a vacation to Turks and Caicos and sent my hippie Uncle Bill and Aunt Kathy over to watch us for a week. They were barely 20 themselves. After four days of hotdogs, I got fed up and went to the grocery store and bought a steak and fried it with butter in a pan for dinner that night. I was eight! My parents were cocktailing and enjoying life while my sister and I were experimenting in the kitchen... with food and with fire. Emptying the freezer and concocting gourmet meals before our treasured TV double shot of *Love Boat* and *Fantasy Island*.

Rifling through my father's dresser drawers, which I tended to do with all family members, I found a silver chain with an interesting leaf medallion. I wore it to school and was immediately seized by my stunned teacher. The "leaf" was that of a marijuana plant, but even more troubling was the fact that it was on the handle of a cocaine spoon. Needless to say, my parents got an embarrassing phone call from school that day. I knew in some ways what it was, but didn't quite care. I wore it anyway. The scolding I received wasn't about what the emblem and spoon meant, but about how I shouldn't go through other people's private things, a lesson I ignored the second my father left the room.

I went through everyone's things. Anyone who I went to visit or see. Related or not. I would tiptoe away and immediately I was in underwear drawers and desktops. I was fascinated by people's things. It gave me insight into their personality more than anything they could ever say. My uncle had a nude magazine drawer a foot deep, which I would sneak to whenever I could. Not just *Playboy*... extremely hardcore stuff. French magazines with people doing strange and wonderful things to one another. But if he noticed one in the wrong place, he'd confront me for snooping around and I'd plead innocence. I got into everyone's business... Uncles, my friends' parents, my parents' friends. I thumbed through paperwork on desks, combed through junk drawers and snooped in carved wooden boxes. I'd make sure to take a mental snapshot so as to return everything to their proper place once I'd thoroughly scanned it over. In the process, I became a kleptomaniac. Pocketed rare coins, stole gold pens, lifted cuff links and generally became a human magnet. My father asked where I got all these things and I told him people gave them to me. Sure, people gave me collectible coins and gold-plated pocketknives. Because I was... sweet... nice? I don't know. Not sure if he believed me, but the excuse was accepted. One summer day I gave my sister's gold necklace to a girl at a snack bar down the street. Such a romantic! Until my sister burst into tears and made me retrieve it.

  My sister used to hang with our next-door neighbor Rebecca, a slouchy, dark-haired tomboy, until they had a falling out. Then one day she knocked on our door and asked for me. She was five years older and pretty nuts. Her whole family was nuts. Her father was a fisherman who worked in the hot sun all day. He was an ex-Marine with an anchor tattooed in the middle of his chest and a perpetual scowl on his face. He'd come home and drink warm Ballentine Ale that he kept on his workbench in the suffocatingly hot garage.

  Rebecca and I became partners in crime... pocketed

everything that wasn't nailed down. Her father gave her 10 bucks to buy some car wax in town, so we went to the store, stole it and spent the money on candy. It was easy... we ripped the security label off and walked out the door. We were the perfect crime couple. Even though I was 10, I looked seven and Rebecca was of an undetermined age and sex – an androgynous tomboy lesbian mashup that you simply didn't notice because she blended into the background.

Browsing the aisles of Toy Town on a snowy Sunday, we stuffed what one might consider grand larceny into our jackets and large wool hats: Space Legos, a hot market item. We'd gained massive amounts of weight since we entered the store, but acted as if there were no wares they could offer that day.

"I think we have to come back another day!" I'd shout, frowning at the junk displayed on the shelves.

"Yea, let's come back later!" Rebecca would echo, as to divert attention to our 20-minute store meander.

As we turned to exit, the manager blocked our path. Arms folded. "Stop!" he commanded. We froze. His face a wall of anger. I was convinced our beautiful reign of shoplifting crime had ended. That was it. The jig was up. Before he said another word, I was thinking of ways to escape my jail cell. "If I could somehow sneak a spoon from the cafeteria, I could loosen a cinderblock beneath my metal cot and dig my way to freedom."

But then his face brightened and he released his crossed arms.

"We're closing early today," he chuckled. "You'll have to come back tomorrow."

We sighed and survived another day.

Unfortunately, my skill at the five-finger-discount was not inherited by others in my immediate age group. While I was stealing candy with my school mate David, he got busted, his skills not as adept as mine. The store clerk called his mother, who came down to the store, dragged him into the parking lot and beat him within an inch of his life. That scene stopped me from stealing... with him. He was terrible, but I continued on with others.

Rebecca and I would run with the neighborhood kids down the street: the Dillon brothers, Dirk and Martin. Two mop-haired blondes with big smiles and eyes. They were pretty progressive for their age. Foul-mouthed, aggressive and armed with X-rated pictures. Dirk was the first homosexual I ever knew. Was open about it at the age of 13. Didn't announce it. Didn't use the word. Didn't have to. While listening to Tainted Love by Soft Cell on his Sony Walkman, he asked me if I had a problem with boys who like other boys. I said no. Case closed.

The Dillons' parents were straight-up swingers. We raided their drawers and closets and uncovered all kinds of bizarre sexual items. Their mother had more vibrators than a Chinese warehouse. Their father had so much porn, his closet could have doubled as an actual porn shop. One magazine he had featured a mustached man cumming on a bald woman's head. The shots were high-quality. Done in a studio on all-white backdrop. That must have been an interesting photo day. I'm not sure what porn category that is. Yul Brynner porn? Alopecia porn? I don't know. Perhaps this was the awakening of my sexual perversions. I always wondered if there was someone else in my family that was a major perv. Unfortunately, no one has stepped forward to stake a claim.

When I was 16, I got arrested with my friends Chip and Bob for breaking into boats at the local boat yard. Living in a harbor town, I could see the boats laid across the land like fat whales, easy to harpoon in the winter. Although we didn't get officially caught with any contraband, we were dragged into the 2nd Precinct by a walrus named Sgt. Spencer. Handcuffed to a table while waiting for our parents to come and beat us senseless, we had the pleasure of berating our table mate... our assistant gym teacher, who got busted for soliciting a prostitute. The fallout was as expected. My mother didn't speak to me for three months. We were all grounded for half a year.

You could chalk this freedom I had to MIA parents. But my parents were there. Often. They just gave me a very long leash. Maybe too long at times. Times were different. Were they better, or just different?

My son is having a good life. He's not raiding the neighbors for porn, but he's having fun. His porn is easy to access now. One click on the iPad and you can watch two girls lick the rim of a cup they just shat in. Back in my day, you had to work hard for your porn! It was like panning for gold. If you didn't trip on something in the back of a shady parking lot, you may find something discarded in a garbage can. But usually you had to dig into your friend's parents closet and when you did, you'd discover all kinds of wonderful things... and you realize that everyone is pretty much a raging pervert.

This is how the generations vary and why they suddenly look down upon each other. We make the world better, or simpler... or more complicated or more difficult so as to be a high-functioning society, then cast blame at one another when the children do exactly as we've planned. The same generation that complained they couldn't set the time on their VCR is also the same generation that made the incredibly complicated personal computer. And somehow that generation can't use computers but explode when their children want to spend all day on them. It's a confounding catch-22 that we seem incapable of escaping from.

    I'm Generation X. The generation that is finally feeling the hangover of the industrial revolution. The "Who's going to clean up this fucking mess?" generation. We're the first generation to not be as financially successful as our parents. It's not possible. The bottom line doesn't go down anymore. The Excel spreadsheet is spread too thin. Unending growth is not a sustainable formula. We're the first generation that saw how the sausage was made... crunched the numbers... calculated the odds and quickly turned... held our hands up in panic to the next generations and screamed "Go back! It's not going to work!"

    Of course, the Boomers thought we ruined everything. It's a rite of passage to blame the generation you created. Luckily, they quickly realize Gen X weren't having any of that nonsense and leapfrogged their ire to Millennials. "What's up with Millennials? Why are they ruining everything?" they say. When older generations toss up their hands and say "I just don't get the generations today," they're admitting they can't remember what they were like 50 years ago. When you look at the scheme of things... the Big Bang and whatnot, that's *not* a very long time! 50 years? A blip on the eternal timeline. Millennials want what everyone else wants... to *not* be replaced by robots. Is that so much to ask? The endless articles about Millennials ruining every industry are laughable.

"Why are Millennials ruining the housing market?" Because children aren't millionaires.

"Why are Millennials ruining the canned meat industry?" Because they can read. It's not hard. Stop it!

The only people who should be confused by other generations are the youth. They're kids. They haven't experienced oldness yet. Old people should be more sympathetic. They've experienced youth. Old folks act as if kids were born with 401k up their ass and constant back pain -- like fighting war and working two jobs -- is a grand rite of passage. Like everyone should do it. As pride. I think kids know pride, toughness and resolve. Try buying a suit for a job interview when you have $20 in your bank account knowing that 1,573 people are applying for the same job. Maybe a bayonet in the face isn't such a bad thing. At least they can see who is sticking it to them. Someone once suggested a reality show where Boomers try and find a job in the modern marketplace with the skills they have, their current resume and current perceptions. Wanna talk about humility? It will drop on you like an Acme anvil. Or worse... get you laughed out of an office building.

My son's generation will inevitably complain about the next generation coming after him and I'm sure they will be based on many of the same problems we have now: screwed-up environment, the cost of living, and how there's no off-planet mining jobs on Mars because it requires a 15-year degree in universe-ology.

I'm not even sure what generation my son is at this point. I think we lost track. We had the Greatest Generation, The Baby Boomers, Generation X, then suddenly there was maybe Generation Z and Millennials? At one point I believe I saw a Y tossed around in there. Someone wasn't really keeping track. Perhaps it's Millennials until the next major milestone... The Kids of WWIII? I don't know. I believe Gen-X named themselves, so perhaps we let it stew in the pot for a while until they figure it out themselves.

One of the character traits that initially bubbled up from Generation X was our discontent at being marketed to... told what to eat and told what to like. When we pushed back and said, "No, we'll like what we want to on our own," the world got upset. Suddenly the world shifted from dictating to being dictated to. That forced people to listen and adapt, which, apparently, is very hard to accept. The new generations can dictate their own fashion, their own loves, their own passions and they can name themselves. We'll all need to listen.

When I found myself at my college graduation from Syracuse U in 1994, I was mesmerized at the commencement speech given by Kurt Vonnegut Jr., the acclaimed author. His speech was excellent. Clever. Funny. Concise. A portion that had always stuck with me was this:

Now you young twerps want a new name for your generation? Probably not, you just want jobs, right? Well, the media do us all such tremendous favors when they call you Generation X, right? Two clicks from the very end of the alphabet. I hereby declare you Generation A, as much at the beginning of a series of astonishing triumphs and failures as Adam and Eve were so long ago.

I apologize. I said I would apologize; I apologize now. I apologize because of the terrible mess the planet is in. But it has always been a mess. There have never been any "Good Old Days," there have just been days. And as I say to my grandchildren, "Don't look at me. I just got here myself."

So, you know what I'm going to do? I declare everybody here a member of Generation A. Tomorrow is another day for all of us.

Generation A -- a visionary concept. Vonnegut gave us an opportunity to move forward as one, even if the plea only fell within earshot. But to dice us all up into the same crockpot to simmer as one meal... old and young... was brilliant.

The times change. They always will. The freedom of the 70s can't be recreated. Neither can the hippie 60s, nor the roaring 20s and a host of other iconic historical moments. But I'm sure my son Max will be part of something weird, wild and wonderful himself. There's new friends out there he has yet to meet, ready to explore the crazy world and discover its hair-raising lunacy. Adventures both amazing and dangerous. Bodies to explore. A vision to follow. A new age of enlightenment. A powerful sonic movement. A futuristic renaissance. A freedom like no one has seen before... one can only dream.

BUGGIN' OUT

12

BUGGIN' 2 ELECTRIC BUGABOO

They say that if you do what you love, you'll never work a day in your life. I'm thankful I don't have a dangerous, mind-numbing labor job like 'sewage tank scrubber' or a 'king's food taster.' When I was a kid, I wanted to be Steven Spielberg... or the *next* Spielberg. What kid doesn't aim for the stars? I thought I had that kind of talent. I believe I do have that kind of talent.

Then you grow up and realize that talent is a fraction of the recipe. Thomas Edison said that genius is 1% inspiration and 99% perspiration, and that's true. But he was also a notorious thief of other inventions, which is a vocation that can get you places if you're good at it. But to be where you want to go, you better be prepared to chef outside the cookbook. Besides a pile of luck... add a dash of crazy, a boatload of risk, a powerful dose of instinct, a healthy portion of connections... and perhaps, if you're so inclined, suck a dick or two.

Growing up, and drawing cartoons, I was told I could be the next Disney... or at least work for them! A lot of people work for Disney... they're called "The Staff." They're all over Disney World. In the cafeteria, in giant animal heads... fine people, all of them.

I parlayed my talents into work and chugged through what I believed to be a series of good decisions. But I looked up one day and found that I was knee-deep in a career that was defining me, wondering where I'm going. The band Talking Heads said it best in their hit song *Once in a Lifetime*... "You may ask yourself; how did I get here?" And to quote musical legend John Lennon, "Life is what happens when you're busy making other plans."

You hear from the Hollywood elite that if you want to be in films, you have to make films yourself. So that's what I did... two of them! I wrote, produced, directed, animated, edited and starred in two animated short films. *Periplanet* and *Periplanet 2*.

Periplanet is about a disillusioned man named Greg who leaves his world behind and walks to the North Pole where he freezes in the tundra. After nuclear war has vaporized the human race, he's unfrozen many years in the future, by the new ruling species of the Earth: the giant cockroach, who command and rule other large insects. The protagonist, who is being caged like an animal, is partnered with a woman named Litka so they can reproduce under the watchful eyes of the bugs. Eventually they escape to the mountains, where they form a new life. It ends with Greg and Litka pregnant, alone and scared.

Periplanet 2 continues the adventures of Greg and Litka, but now they have children, Kim and Xander. One day, while exploring and running from roaches, they stumble upon a race of humanoid underground dwellers called the Obs. The family partners with the Obs underground until they are flushed out by the roaches riding giant Praying Mantises. The group escapes to the surface, but they're surrounded... only to be rescued by Clay-To, a black Englishman in silver knight armor who swoops down on a battalion of Fireflies, electrocutes the Mantis and frees the group. He then invites them to live in Antarctica, which is now warm and habitable.

I'm proud of the films... spent decades batting them around my brain. Eventually, I worked up the nerve to spend my hard-earned money to make them. I spent precious time and energy producing them and putting them out into the world. I painstakingly wrote all the scripts, did all the backgrounds, designed the characters, recorded the voices, structured the sound design, created animation rigs and did a lot of the animation myself... hired and directed animators from all over the world... Argentina, Brazil, Spain, New Zealand and Tennessee. I helped score the music, played some music myself even though I'm not a musician and did all the advertising, graphic design and promotions. I've constructed complicated world-building, scenarios and storylines both for the current films and for the films I'm planning for the future. Relationships, eventual character introductions, love stories, and of course, countless giant colorful bugs. I have notebooks packed with thoughts, ideas, sketches, printouts and concepts. I pored over the details and poured my blood, sweat and tears into the films... and, most importantly, I sacrificed sleep and precious time away from my family working on them. I consider the films good. The second one I'd consider excellent. Artistically I think they're satisfying. Instead of wondering "what if?" my whole life, I made them and put them out in the world. They're no longer in my head. They're out! On the internet. They're the world's to enjoy... or piss on.

But they garnered no acclaim. No interest. No success in terms of propelling me forward in the field of film or animation. They sit like a frog on a log by a speeding highway. Never to be seen unless a Hollywood producer breaks down and sees them on the side of the road. And even then, would the producer sit long enough to see the frog? You'd have to look at the frog for a chunk of time, and in today's world, if you're not a frog that gives up the goods within 10 seconds, the producer is gone. I hate frogs.

So, I'm left to promote my talent on my own. Represent myself. Which is like doing brain surgery on yourself. Where do you start? The internet! Within seconds you realize it's futile. I mean the representing myself part; self-brain surgery is self-explanatory. Like the old lawyer adage: A person who represents themselves in a court of law has a fool for a client. So, it's abandoned immediately. I'm no fool. I spent money paying for hits on YouTube and Facebook, but the attention span of the average human these days is apparently 3.5 seconds, so asking someone to sit idle and watch a 15-minute animated film is like asking them to learn molecular cell biology.

My next thought is my brother-in-law's brother and good friend, Charlie. I had it in my head that he could be my agent. Or my manager. Or whatever the hell it is you need to get a foot in the door... a handler? Zookeeper? Whatever it is, I need one. But where's Charlie? Do you know what Charlie is up to these days? The truth is I don't. No one does, really. Not even his brother; my sister's husband. I haven't talked to Charlie in a year. He's living on the east end of Long Island in Montauk and generally practicing the art of being a recluse. Apparently, he did law school, but no one's sure if he graduated... or if he's practicing law. Or what the hell he's doing at all. That kind of disappearing act is to be admired. If you're going to drop out, might as well go all in. Many people work hard for that kind on anonymity.

Charlie had the acting bug at one time, so he knows the passion of wanting to get in the biz. He's smart in business, knows the law and knows how to get things done... at least that is the perception I attributed to him as I lick Cheetos dust off my fingers from the confines of my comfy office chair. For all I know, he's clueless in regard to anything. But I doubt it, as I've seen him figure out complex documents for me when I needed him in a jam, getting my wife and I through green card papers. He's a big guy with a big personality with a jovial presence and a hearty laugh. If you banged out a screenplay on your 1950s typewriter of a talent agent, you'd most likely get a version of Charlie. How he hid for so long is beyond my understanding. But if you want to play hide and seek, the world is a pretty big playground. I've had daydreams of him as my agent. Those thoughts usually popped up in the shower between my imaginary interviews with Conan O'Brien and Anderson Cooper.

"I hear you're with your amazing agent tonight, Is

that right, A.J.?"

"That's right Conan, my agent Charlie, right over there." The camera spins around and Charlie waves. Conan shouts, "Give it up for Charlie, ladies and gentlemen!" as the crowd roars in adoration.

So, after years of sitting on the notion of Charlie becoming my agent, I wrote him an email. It was a long, philosophical email more like the ravings of a madman. I wrote about life and how it's ticking away – that we won't live forever and that we should grab life and live it to its fullest. That he and I be one as partners; attacking Hollywood with the zeal of swashbucklers. I proceeded to sit on that email for months, revising it and updating it until I worked up the courage to send it. Click!

•••

It's been crickets on Charlie's end. I wrote him months ago, but nothing. Granted, I dropped an anvil on him. After I read the email again, I realize I pulled the pin on a live grenade and lobbed it over... hoping he'd respond in kind. Perhaps his kind response was to filter the email into the trash. So, I move on alone. It's the easiest way. Even if he's gung-ho about the proposal, I'm preparing for the worst. Like I always am. I've mentally prepared for the worst of everything... a shooting at my son's school, my wife's impending cancer, the car accident where I'm t-boned by an Amazon delivery truck and die a slow death in the hospital, cursing myself for not creating 'life wisdom' videos that my son can find on the computer so he still has *something* of me to hold onto decades from now. He'll fire up my old Mac desktop computer... a new model now, but in a few short years it will be as relevant as a Ford Model-T. He'll double click a .mov file titled "Papa video 1" and I'll spring up in still frame. The image of my face in awkward mid-word under the play arrow. "Hi Max" I'd say... roaring fire in the background of a cozy study as I clench a walnut pipe in my teeth... red silk robe. You've seen the set-up... something you probably watched on some kind of PBS story hour hosted by a British guy you saw playing a British guy on some British show with other British people with British accents. I'd close the giant leather-bound book I was pretending to read, spout brilliant words of wisdom. None of them my own, of course. I have a lot of philosophies about life living in my head, but when I try to conflate them into a coherent message, I simply blurt out "Just Do It" which is unoriginal and trademarked by a company already.

Because Charlie has decided to ignore me, maybe even disown me as a family member, I turn my attention to the most logical person I can think of... George Lucas. I write him a letter and ship it off to some compound in the sleepy wine country of California. Believe it or not, I didn't hear from him either! That's because he's too busy sleeping in huge piles of cash and has sunken so deep inside them, no one can reach him with fresh mail unless they repel down with ropes and cables.

Here's my letter to George Lucas for the hell of it...

Dear Mr. Lucas,
I'm writing to you because I don't know who else to turn to. I know, I'm turning to one of the most famous people on the planet Earth, but I figured, perhaps, that you'd be able to help a frustrated and talented animator and filmmaker...me.

Of course, I'm a huge fan of Star Wars. I saw the film in the theater when I was 5, and I dressed as Indiana Jones every day in seventh grade for about a month. Yes, I was made fun of, but people thought it was actually quite cool because... who didn't like Indiana Jones in 1984? But I'm writing to you because I'm actually a big fan of one of your more recent films... the wonderful Strange Magic. I truly think it's just a lovely animated film. Gorgeous to look at with stunning visuals. Perhaps the story wasn't what anyone wanted at the time, but I think it's really magical.

It's the reason I'm writing to you.

I've been working for the better part of two decades on a concept that I've poured blood, sweat, tears, and yes, money into. It's a series of animated films called PERIPLANET.

They are about a disillusioned man who leaves New York and walks to the North Pole where he freezes to death. After the world collapses under nuclear war, he's awoken from his frozen slumber by the next rulers of the world... the insects.

Like the dinosaurs, then the humans... the insects will inherit the Earth in my vision.

I've made two animated short films based on this concept so far:
PERIPLANET & PERIPLANET 2

They are available on YouTube if you care to seek them out. I'm in the process of doing a third film titled... PERIPLANET 3.

If this letter somehow by the grace of the United States Postal Service (and God) reaches you, through all the 5,000 pieces of mail you get a day... I'd love for you to consider helping me get the PERIPLANET concept to a bigger market.

I simply don't know how to get into the film business and I'm not sure I ever will without some help. I have little connections and the world works in such odd ways. I can't get anyone to even look at the films, let alone buy into the world building I've created.

Perhaps you're bored and looking for some creative outlets. Don't worry! I'll do all the tedious work. But your thoughts and influence would be greatly appreciated.

If this letter is lost in the paperwork of time, know through the winds... or osmosis, that I think you are a genius and when you left the Star Wars universe in the hands of other people, the world lost a visionary artist who is beyond compare...

I hope you are happy and well.

With all sincerity,
A.J. Schmitz

    This is an actual letter I sent to George Lucas at the age of 47. Now, I've been known to stretch the truth to emphasize an argument or to curry favor to a view I'm trying to support. Sometimes I'll go full-bore to the extreme to really hammer the point home. Saying I've been waiting in line for five minutes will not generate the sympathy I hope to evoke like saying I've been waiting in line for NINE HOURS. That will really pull the heart strings. But it's not just the exaggeration, it's the carefully chosen words. The word nine has a harder edge than using the number eight or eleven. It spikes into your heart. That's why when a German says NO, it really feels like the end of an argument.

    So, I stretch the truth. Yes, it's true, I did dress like Indiana Jones in the seventh grade. But it wasn't for a month. I dressed like Indiana Jones for like... a year and a half. I know. It's awkward to think about. My parents even bought me a genuine leather whip for Christmas one year. I'd practice snapping at the posters on my bedroom walls, creating exciting gashes across the legs of Heather Thomas in her hip-hugging hot pink bikini. It was such a prolonged and deep absorption, it bordered on a living art piece. It eventually became so detailed, I progressed into the *Temple of Doom* phase, removing the leather jacket and tearing the sleeve off my beige safari shirt, exposing my entire right arm. Then I wrapped my fingers in dirty bandages, blasted the shirt open to my navel and calmly paraded around the house with a machete in case I came across a rope bridge to sever.

I toned down the Indy Jones thing in my letter so as not to appear to be a total kook. Sure, fan mail from a full-grown, even borderline *old* man, begging to help him with his animated movie is crazy, but to show documentation of a history of crazy is to send a red flag not only to them, but most likely the FBI as well. The part where I did stretch the truth was in my praise of the film *Strange Magic*. It's a clunker. Beautifully animated, no doubt. It's a gorgeous film to look at. But boy is it a hackneyed piece of stupid. I know I used the word wonderful, but if forced to pinpoint *where* it's wonderful, I'm sure I can angle the argument to a few places. Still, I'm surprised George didn't read the letter and dash from his cushy lair and hop a redeye flight to New York to shake my hand. Missed opportunity for him. If George reads this now, he'll know I lied. I have no doubt he'll immediately cut the funding on all my animated projects.

•••

I return home from Home Depot with a shitload of glue traps to catch the Camel Crickets that are hopping around the house. When cooler weather comes upon us, the bugs like to come inside. For a man who made animated short films about bugs, I sure spend a lot of time trying to eliminate them. Personally, I like bugs. They're fascinating... little armored creatures crawling around the earth. Tiny villages all over the planet that we crush with our feet. My family, on the other hand, can't stand them. And if you ever had a Camel Cricket bouncing around your house, you know the terror my family is going through. Camel Crickets are like something out of a horror movie.

As I approach my home office desk, I spot a folded manila envelope with LUCASFILM printed on a white label. My heart jumps. I think the envelope may have glowed while angels sang. It's been half a year since I wrote George. But upon closer inspection, the label may actually have been printed on an old dot matrix printer from 1985 with the perforated guide holes on the side you pull off when finished. Looks no more professional than an amateur kidnapper's ransom note. Inside though, is the warm and tender letter from George Lucas that I was expecting...

Dear A.J.,

George Lucas is retired... blah blah blah... He sold the company to Disney... Yadda yadda. He doesn't do this shit anymore... blah blah. We don't accept ideas without representation... etc. etc. Please cease and desist sending us more crap without representation... and so on.

Just the response I was hoping for! I'm considering hanging the letter on my wall... starting a new rejection mosaic like I did years prior. The letter is attached to my original letter which was sent back to me... thrown right back in my face.

I guess I'm on my own. See! I do need my brother-in-law, Charlie. Unfortunately, I haven't heard from him yet... Maybe I'll see him at Christmas where I can confront him face-to-face. Until then, I'll start the process of doing *Periplanet 3* on my own. Create another GoFundMe page that everyone will ignore and collect some small cash donations to start with... get the ball rolling. I do have one major fan though... my son, Maximilian. He asks me constantly when I'm going to make *Periplanet 3*. I tell him I'm going to start any day now.

But I don't want to paint a Norman Rockwell picture here. My son isn't a sweet, completely unobjectionable fan of his Papa. He's been as critical as anyone to what I've created. Although he's watched the movies multiple times... generally because he likes them, his critiques of the movies have ranged from "They're OK, they're not great" to "Why does it sound like my voice was recorded in a bathroom?" That's true love right there... or a child's unencumbered raw view. But now the time has come. Fall is here, winter is coming and it's the perfect time to start an indoor creative project. The script is written, the storyboards are completed... I just need to dive headfirst into the tough stuff.

My wife is already rolling her eyes.

BUGGIN' OUT

13

FOOTLOCKER TREASURES
PART II - THE SEQUEL

The fascinating separation of the abdomen from the thorax gave us a clear understanding of the internal skeletal morphological system. My classmate Scott and I had just finished carefully dissecting the honeybee, beaming with pride about the meticulous work. Still, our teacher stood over us with an obvious glare of disapproval. Mostly because this was a high school Spanish class. Our focus on the bee drew the focus of the other students, and that was not how a Spanish class worked.

A month before, I was in a different Spanish class. I remember walking into *that* class and thinking "Hey! This is great, bunch of people I rarely see in class. Some jocks, popular kids and some pretty girls." That's because it was AP Spanish... for smart people. After a few days, a scheduling counselor crashed through the door mid-lesson and announced I was in the wrong class. My fellow students bid me farewell with a chorus of snickers as I was steered into the direction of the class next door. Passing Gary in the hallway, who it seemed was *also* in the wrong class and was being steered *into* AP Spanish by another counselor, I entered my rightful place... the world of the perpetual C– student. Those of us the teachers taught *at*, and not *to*. Like robots programmed to keep going, these teachers persevered regardless of who was paying attention or what object was being tossed at their head. These were my people... the tolerated, the stupid... the drooling, huddled masses, swinging from the tree. The bee dissection is what one might call resourceful learning. You're presented with high school Spanish, but you turn to entomology to help the crushing boredom. I'm sure my science class consisted of more Spanish than Spanish class, but I wouldn't know because I wasn't paying attention in science class either. Math can be music, English can be writing, and every class can be art if all you do is doodle in notebooks. At Syracuse University, I studied advertising and graphic design and received a BFA in those fields. That much is true. But one of the most interesting classes I took was one I designed myself.

During my college days in Syracuse in the early 1990s, there were two distinct malls. The newly-built Carousel Mall, constructed on the grounds of a toxic waste dump, and the older, smaller Shoppingtown Mall, where I was gainfully employed at a vitamin store aptly named Vitamin World. Although Shoppingtown had a carousel and was not built on a toxic dump, it was demoted by proxy as the forgotten bastard of malls, standing in the shadow of the spangling new Carousel Mall. The only reason I got the Vitamin World job was because the manager knew Pat Fitzmaurice, a guy I painted houses with for years, and because Shoppingtown Mall was desperate for anyone to come and work or shop there as the seldom visited, second-rate mall. To obtain the job and be an effective salesman, I had to learn all about vitamins and how each worked in correlation to one another... the delicate vitamin dance. Yet when customers entered the store, all that knowledge was tossed out the window and I'd tout the magical healing powers of vitamins like a snake oil salesman. Any patron who equated a disorder with its potential vitamin cure was met with immediate agreement from me.

"Is Vitamin A good for the sciatic nerve? You sir, have been doing your research!" Filling their arm with bottles, I'd continue on... "You know what else is good for that nerve thing? Vitamin D, Selenium, Potassium and Inositol. That will be 87 dollars."

My new college class syllabus, created by me, deemed I live on an 18-hour schedule (6 hours sleep, 12 hours awake). In some class, my buddy Kevin Sherwood read about a scientist who found this 18-hour schedule to be a more efficient lifestyle. According to this genius, the human brain and body functioned at a superior level on this clock system... the rotation of the earth be damned. Without doing a second of research on this guy, I dove into this experiment head-first.

Sure enough, as I ventured deeper into the 18-hour cycle, I became a highly functioning individual. I was razor-sharp... my brain limber and my body well-rested. It was going swimmingly until I found myself falling asleep at 2:00 in the afternoon and waking up at 8:00 at night. I compensated for the lag by raiding the shelves of Vitamin World... experimenting with herb combinations like Yohimbe and Gingko Biloba. My blood vessels opened and there was the occasional surprise boner, but that happened during my normal drug and drinking routine anyway. Not even heavy doses of vitamin C, which came in a delicious, citrusy 1000mg chewable tablets, seemed to help. Why I believed supplements would solve complex time management issues, I can't say. Two weeks into the experiment, the class was dissolved. I found it challenging to get six billion people onto the same groove I was riding on. I did however have remarkably fresh breath as we sold breath mints that were infused with real mint and parsley.

    My favorite class in college, not created by me, was Jazz history. If you visited any dental office from 1977 to 1982, you were bound to hear the sweet wailing flugelhorn of Chuck Mangione and his smash hit, *Feels So Good*. My class was taught by his piano-playing older brother, Gap Mangione. It's easy to shoot a squirrel, and I assume just as easy to gut and tan its pelt, because that's what Gap tried to pass-off as a hairpiece. An enthusiastic and inspiring teacher, Gap would explain jazz music with passion, jumping on the available upright piano to bang out notes while spoon-feeding us easy to digest jazz history. One snowy day, he played a record of Louis Armstrong's *I got a Right to Sing the Blues*. Recollecting listening to the song in his family's parlor with Chuck as children, he burst into tears and rushed from the room, rendering the half-stoned class speechless. He returned apologizing, embarrassed and flustered, wiping tears from his eyes. To me, it was the finest moment I'd ever had with a teacher... showing the power of music.

    Forgoing a very clear set of criteria for graduating, I took any class I desired that was offered. I painted with the restricted senior painting class because I asked them to let me in. I took sculpture and an early form of computer animation. I took science fiction film history, as well as other odd curriculum like music editing. Nearing the end of the line of my educational journey, the advertising department head called me into her office and produced evidence that I'd not really studied advertising at the highest level. That maybe, I'd taken some liberties with the curriculum, missed some required classes and often went outside the field of art in general. I feigned ignorance... "Huh? Really?" So, we fudged some numbers, made things apply and I graduated with a BFA In Advertising and Design.

I had a huge crush on a theater major named Ashley who I finally asked out. While walking to a restaurant on a date, I smoothly flipped my arm over her head and onto her shoulder. At least, that's how I planned it in my head. In reality, I elbowed her in the ear and knocked her earring out... a shining example of my success with women in college. I wasn't very confident and after a while, I gave up dating and threw myself into people's film projects. I starred in some films and floundered through minor parts in others. At the class of '93's senior film showcase, I was in about 50% of the films, which became comical after a while. Without being a film major, I was as versed in film and ensconced in the film program as much as anyone.

Back at the footlocker in my workshop, I uncover *Universal Taxi*, my directorial debut. It's the only movie I have that's actually film on a reel. Black and white. I yank the strip and hold it up to the light. It's as poorly made as I remember. Shitty film quality, bad lighting, cheap set design... the list goes on. Also inside the footlocker are various plastic VHS tapes filled with my college film history. The cases are dusty and stiff and the labels I designed and printed on my cheap inkjet printer, mimicking VHS covers you'd see in a Blockbuster video, are peeling off in curls. Along with the story descriptions, I wrote faux reviews with every film receiving "Two Thumbs Up" from Siskel and Ebert. The various cover styles represent my life in amateur student filmmaking and even more amateurish graphic design. There's a fleeting thought to transfer them to a digital movie file, but the price tag is undoubtedly more than I care to pay. Some of the films were professionally transferred to VHS tapes at the time. Most of the film students were broke by year's end and couldn't afford to have their films professionally transferred, so they'd project the film on a wall and record it with a camcorder. Not only is it a terrible reproduction with poor visuals and even worse sound quality, but the technique doesn't hold up well over time.

  I haven't owned a VCR since Barrack Obama was a senator, but my father's basement man-cave entertainment system is an electronics museum. When I come by to borrow his VCR, he's happy to tell me he only paid $25 dollars for it, but also stresses that its timely return would be appreciated. Apparently, they don't make VCRs anymore and they're as rare as Dodo birds. It's also cast an unsightly clean spot on the cabinet's dusty faux wooden shelf, which will serve as a constant reminder of its notable absence.

  I watch these film gems with my son in what I believe will be hilarious bonding moment between us, but I'm met with ghastly confusion on his end. This kid was raised in 4K and the film quality is so poor, the production values slowly sap the joy from him. His astuteness of film is also very high, so every creative choice is scorned and leads to endless questions.

"How old is this?"

"Why does it look so bad?"

"Were you trying to make a bad movie?"

But we get through the mini-film-fest regardless, watching the movies in order of their creation...

JACK (1991) Directed by Brian Stranko

The film opens with me getting punched in the face. I crash against a brick wall and slide down, crumpling to the ground in a heap. I play Jack, a low-level gangster and punching bag. A mob boss (Kevin) and his cronies hover over me in a shot from my POV. One of them (Brian) is chained like a dog and sniffs curiously over me. They demand that I get them the money I owe, "Or else!"

This shot was filmed in a dank Syracuse alleyway that was also a prime cut-through for drunk students on their way home to hurl in their toilets. We were tripped-over multiple times and production was halted throughout the night because we had to explain to these magically materializing thespians why we couldn't allow them in front of the camera for a monologue.

Later in the film, Jack is awoken and scooped up by a nameless janitor, who takes him into his workplace dungeon to nurse him back to health. Played by Kevin's roommate,

John, the janitor squeals his way through a series of hick philosophies. John compounds his own South Carolina accent by screeching each line in the back of his throat in the most grating tone imaginable, making the film almost unwatchable. I have one line in the film, which benefits the film because I'm unable to push out more than a hush with my weak projection. Needless to say, we're untrained actors.

The film climaxes with Jack finding a diamond ring the janitor has lying around... like most janitors do! Jack snatches the ring off the ground and pockets it, but the janitor senses what's going on. Being too stupid to realize the diamond's worth, or perhaps is so content to sweep shit all day and clueless to life's capitalistic system, he lets Jack have the ring. On final cut, Brian leaves a monotone synthesizer hum drone-on as Jack bolts down the alley, diamond ring in hand, to pay his debts. Brian insists he'll remove the synth hum, but I like it and tell him to keep it, which he does. The synth hum turns out to be the film teacher's favorite part of the movie. Brian is incredulous.

DEATH (1991) Directed by Kevin Sherwood

An experimental film collage... Me with coins over my eyes, me entering the men's room in slow-motion. Me in front mirrors showcasing confusing perspectives. Me washing my face, walking the streets and generally existing in shots that can be interpreted by anyone as anything. They are well done... I give a riveting performance. I believe there's a girl in it. I read letters. My son Max has endless questions, which forces me to explain a completely unexplainable movie.

UNIVERSAL TAXI (1993) Directed by A.J. Schmitz

The first film I directed. Kevin plays a taxi dispatcher on Earth who notifies me, a taxi driver in space, that I need to pick up a ride. Using crude clay models, bad lighting, black mounting boards flecked with white paint dots to represent stars in space, and other flimsy practical effects, I construct, as best I could, a film in which I'm zipping through the cosmos in a space taxicab. I eventually cross paths with a floating spaceman (also played by Kevin) who magically appears in the backseat of my cab. He removes his helmet and blinds with me with light. It's a metaphor of sorts, I'm sure.

2001: A Space Odyssey, it is not. Channeling Scooby-Doo's Thelma, my Israeli teacher, who had hard-on for Leni Riefenstahl, gave me a B on the film for my imagination. But the melding of real people and clay models doesn't jell and suspension of disbelief is nearly impossible. I should note that this movie was completed and released four years before *The 5th Element*. Fuck you, Luc Besson.

BLOODVISIONS (1993) Directed by Brian Stranko

Since the Lumière Brothers first projected images onto a screen in 1895, there have been both wild successes and unmitigated disasters in the annals of film history. Box office smashes so big, they've made mere mortals into gods, and bombs so large, they've bankrupted major studios. Many films have gone down in history for their stranger-than-fiction backstories... *Apocalypse Now*, *Fitzcarraldo*, *Heaven's Gate*, *The Man Who Killed Don Quixote*. Cast and crew in-fighting, set designs destroyed by nature, actors stomping off sets. Budget issues and studio heads snatching negatives from directors. *Bloodvisions* has all that and more. What was slated to be an epic 45-minute senior horror film became a horribly misconstrued runaway train that, at final cut, was a confusing and unsatisfying 12 minutes.

Brian spent an entire year working on the film. Sleepless nights, endless days toiling away in a darkened editing room, working with a budget higher than anyone else in the class, pissing away money he didn't have.

The film starred, me, your humble narrator as Jack (of course), a disillusioned man working as a clown to make ends meet. One day, while drinking booze in an alley, Jack gets bitten in the neck by a rat, which rats are known to do. Unfortunately, we never see the rat because our pet rat Fred, who was slated to co-star, escaped his plastic cage and never appeared in the film. To compensate the lack of Fred, I merely flinch and spasm to simulate being bitten by a rat, which confuses the viewer completely as it looks like I'm having an ordinary seizure. There's almost no exposition to the whole sequence, so it's incredibly odd. The flask of whiskey I'm pulling from does however fall, and its potent brown liquid dribbles into the snow, alluding to the coming blood issues, if you're able to pick up on such imagery.

As time goes on, Jack's attitude declines from alleyway booze-guzzling, disgruntled clown, to just plain strange... lashing out at his wife, eating raw meat from the fridge and eventually turning pale and growing fangs. I spend a good chunk of the movie dressed as a clown vampire, which I suppose was a melding of the horror genre's two significant imageries that terrify people. This acting clay, when molded by my hands, quickly becomes a crooked ashtray.

Overcome by hunger one evening, I threaten to eat our new baby, played perfectly by Brian's new baby sister Chloe. From my deranged hallucinating perspective, the baby is so appetizing that she appears on a bed of lettuce. This is meant to be a surreal and twisted moment in the film, but comes across with as much subtlety as Wile E. Coyote licking his chops over a rotisserie Roadrunner mirage.

Before I can dig into the baby, a robber (Brian) breaks in and desperately combs the place for contraband. While hiding, I watch in the shadows as the robber contemplates stealing fiberglass insulation... the scene being shot in our barren attic, where there's nothing to steal. When Jack thinks the baby is being threatened, he lashes out. In self-defense, the robber threatens to cut the baby and I turn from daddy to diner and maul the thug in a vicious neck-biting scene. Jack's wife arrives and absorbs the bloody carnage in a long pan shot, so she snatches the baby and hits Jack in the foot with a hammer, chasing me from the house where I eventually live on the outskirts of town.

Meanwhile, a crew of scientists are tracking me, working in conjunction with the crazed local anti-clown/vampire sheriff who's got a hankerin' for some justice. Later, I violently return to kill, but I'm captured in a net by the scientist/sheriff posse and studied in a lab. Strapped to an examination table, I have flashbacks, which send me into a rage. I break from my restraints and go for the sheriff's jugular in a gory bloodletting. At that point, I turn to the camera and hiss, letting the viewer know that I'm too far gone to be saved. In a twist of irony, I'm shot dead by my wife, who still loves me, using the sheriff's gun, which slid to her feet in the melee.

Once assembled at full length, it's an absolute howler of a film. Just a disaster. *Plan 9 From Outer Space* bad. Of the films many problems, the sheriff was played by a chubby local actor named Ricky, who longed to be famous by plowing through dinner theater around Syracuse. Ricky yanked his falling pants up in every shot and somehow channeled our friend John's excruciatingly shrill southern accent from Brian's film *Jack*. It essentially kills the movie. His scenes are so atrocious, Brian is forced to cut him from the film until the end, when his neck becomes vampire dinner.

Of course, now the movie doesn't make much sense because the scenes where the scientists are hunting Jack, using instruments like old TVs that double as science devices, hit the cutting room floor as well. A great scene, where I come smashing through the front door of our house, where we took the front door off the hinges of our actual house and replaced it with a fake door that I really smashed through, also hits the cutting room floor. I nearly dislocated my shoulder doing it, but I have passion for the film, so I was all in.

I had spray painted my hair black for the movie, so it's unnaturally stark. Our makeup artist was all in at the beginning, but once her own movie became unwieldy (they all do) I was left to do the makeup myself, with varying degrees of continuity success.

What remains of the film is basically me, crawling around in a clown onesie with giant pom-pom buttons on the front, looking similar to Ewan McGregor in *Trainspotting* -- except with fangs and less acting pedigree.

The film is now a 12-minute collage of voice-overs, sweeping camera movements, hard to grasp motivations, and random scenes of me acting like a maniac out of context. It barely makes sense and it's a shell of the ultimate vision and the stunning amount of time we put into the production doesn't show on screen. Even at 12 minutes it's a howler of a movie with the pièce de résistance being a long crane shot scene where I crawl up the stairs, into the baby's room and push my face into the playpen netting, hungry for blood.

If anything, I learned a great deal about film on this production. Mostly, how things can go terribly, terribly wrong very easily. If you add a few million dollars to Brian's budget, or even tens of millions of dollars to the budget, a good idea can go off the rails very quickly and one can see why people can lose their jobs, and their shirts, in the film industry. And when time is a factor, you can't go back. The runaway train just plows through the wall and everyone in the area gets knocked in all directions like bowling pins.

TOLL (1994) Directed by Jason Lycette

This is my student film swan song. I play a toll booth operator manning the toll of a lonely road in the middle of nowhere. I do things to kill the boredom like roll up paper balls and play basketball in a brown paper lunch bag and dance terribly to songs on the radio. Each night, the same woman comes to the toll. She barely cracks the window because she's shy (supposedly) and feeds a dollar through the window slit. In reference to the window height, I say charming lines like "I won't bite" which is like catnip to women in the movies. Each time she comes, she engages in more and more conversation, rolling her window down a little more each time. Finally, at the end, she has the courage to roll the window completely down to meet me face to face. The audience sees the actress for the first time. But I've been replaced with a coin basket. A tragedy. It's a pretty good movie. Simple. A bit cliché, but it shows what a decent movie can be with a simple concept, some timely music and just two characters.

We filmed the movie at an abandoned toll booth situated on the south campus that once manned a parking lot, but had long since been defunct. What parking the lot provided was not clear, as it was a lot with no accompanying building within site. What it did provide was brutal, unforgiving winds. Without trees or any coverage, the booth stood naked for the elements to hammer without relenting. The booth itself was a dream for the movie as it was unobstructed, unused and unoccupied. The camera, lights and crew moved freely around it without care. Unfortunately, I was not free to move without care because my joints were locked into place like frozen steaks. We filmed at night, in the middle of winter, where blasting frigid winds nearly drove us into hypothermia. The story took place in another time and location... a land of fairy tales even. My costume, other than pants, was a collared shirt and nametag. Yet the heavy clouds of breath billowing around my face would tell a different story... a story where a toll booth operator lived in the tundra, yet decided to wear the clothing of toll booth operator living in a place like Florida.

We ran a generator for lights and warmth, but that was moved about 100 yards away to prevent the engine noise from recording onto the sound mix. That worked, but what didn't work was getting the car engine noise off the sound mix. The rumbling engine as it pulled up to the booth, blocked my already stated weak projection, as well as my chattering teeth. Somehow, we never thought to cut the engine for close-up dialogue and the engine rumbling makes poor acting wash away in mumbling.

I would perform in a few other films my final year, the last being an experimental art film directed by a girl I liked who wanted to shoot in a found-objects sculpture park in the glorious hamlet of Munnsville. It was the land of Delbert Ward, a man accused of killing his brother only a few years prior. That murder story, detailed in a documentary titled *Brother's Keeper*, would capture the strange world of the brothers and their dark mysterious lives *inside* the Ward home. The experimental art film starring me, would capture all the beauty of rotting wood windows that framed doll heads and car parts that hung from trees, *outside* the Ward home. A natural botanical weed garden, the place gave off a vibe consistent with nightmares and missing people. I was filmed in various sets... walking and standing, at times clothed and shirtless, among assorted rusting backdrops and the occasional serendipitous fluttering dove. These are films created by people who follow a non-linear path of filmmaking. The cinematographers, the visual artists... the untalented writers.

BUGGIN' OUT

14

CANDY FLIPPING WITH THE DEAD

On my skinny, ten-year-old skull, the enormous white bubble headphones looked like two refrigerators glued to the sides of my head. The thick, black, phone-like cord jammed into the complicated glowing Hi-Fi gave me the appearance of an air-traffic controller landing a spaceship down runway 54. I discovered the beauty of music on my father's stereo system, listening to scratchy, poppy Beatles records. Not a bad place to start in the life-cycle of music education. I'd listen to his crackling vinyl albums for hours and hours... the Rolling Stones, Stevie Wonder, The Doors and ABBA until MTV fed me a steady diet of just about anyone they could jam into a music video. Eventually the Ramones, Elvis Costello, The Pixies and the sweet sounds of Public Enemy seeped in till I was a devoted music lover of all genres. But one group I never seemed to acquire a taste for, no matter how many attempts I made to listen, was The Grateful Dead.

This sentiment drew the ire of many of my family

members and a small chunk of close friends. My uncles were *huge* Deadheads, which was evident by the posters occupying every square inch of their bedroom walls. Skeletons wearing crowns of roses, skeletons with top hats, skeletons smoking cigarettes, skeletons with one eye socket and skeletons walking in desert landscapes. It seemed everything they owned was in dedication to the Dead. I could never understand the obsession.

Every time I heard that distinctive Grateful Dead plinking, it sounded like the same song... and that song consisted of Jerry Garcia tuning a complicated guitar while droning on about going somewhere he wanted to go... I assumed to the desert with a cigar-smoking skeleton. I honestly could not decipher between any song in their catalog, although they seemed to have hundreds of songs because my uncles had countless records with skeletons on them. They also traded live shows on cassette tapes that were meticulously documented... Anaheim, 84... Frankfurt, 79.... every destination the band could drop their gear and set up a stage. Each cassette had an unfathomable list of songs scribbled in tiny writing that threatened to run off the case into a void. My college buddy had thousands of cassette tape recordings and I couldn't imagine when he had time to listen to them all. To listen to all the tapes he possessed, while receiving new tapes, would require more time than was humanly possible. He'd need to be three people with eight ears and at least two brains. It was a space-time, and human body-part conundrum.

The Dead were notorious for having some of the most successful concert tours in music history. For 20+ years, their concerts were completely sold out from California to Australia, and the crazed hippie kids who gobbled mind-expanding drugs could always be found following their favorite merry minstrels... searching for a ticket to ride. My personal experience came at the end of June in 1995. My friend Ian called and surprised me with extra tickets to see The Dead at Giants Stadium in the Meadowlands. I never really thought much about The Dead, but it was probably the only opportunity I'd have to see them. My uncles and cousins followed them around for years before they ran out of money and gas, kicked booze and drugs, or simply had families. This would be my chance to see what all the fuss was about and perhaps, finally, make me a convert.

The day started at noon on a balmy Saturday. Ian, tall and lanky with sandy hair that framed his sharp smile, loaded my silver Volvo station wagon with a cooler of Meister Brau beer and enough weed and mind-altering treats to last us through a nuclear winter. I wore a button-down shirt purchased from a yard sale that looked like an oil slick had spilt into a batch of fluffy clouds. I complemented that with a ratty straw hat. Ian wore a pair of bright orange Converse All Stars. I know he wore more, but that's all my hazy memory can recall.

We were to rendezvous with some others at a gas station and drive convoy-style to the Meadowlands, where glassy-eyed babes would be wandering aimlessly for spare tickets and the meaning of life. My breakfast and the hot weather alone were enough to twist my brain into a tie-dyed puddle, when we met our fellow concert-going mates. I couldn't tell you now who those people were or what they looked like, but they all seemed nice enough. But instead of a convoy, everyone piled into the Volvo and Ian took the wheel. We cruised down the LIE at a good clip while smoking joints and swigging cold orange juice. The cops were out in record force as a Grateful Dead show was always cause for alarm by the state and local 'peace officers.' You know how savage those hippie bastards can get. Some of them have been known to drive too slowly or show enthusiastic amounts of caring.

Ian channeled his inner pharmacist, taking care of all the necessary drugs, which he dispensed to us with proper timing and care. "We'll take the Ecstasy now" he said reassuringly, "and when that kicks in we'll drop the acid." After an hour had passed, the Ecstasy kicked in nicely. I began to understand the rotation of the earth as one of our fellow companions strummed his guitar in the back seat. As the Manhattan skyline came into view, Ian started bellowing about *Braveheart*, which he'd just seen in the theater. His diatribe consisted of how the flesh was stronger than steel and before I knew it, he was practically bending the steering wheel with his open palm. It seemed to make perfect sense at the time.

But I'll never be quite sure as I was breaking the 69th Street Bridge down into miniature fibers and analyzing them with numbers. He ended his tirade with "Fuck it, I don't know" as we glided into Manhattan. In the Lincoln Tunnel, Ian handed us the acid, which he assured us would rock our world. The club kids called the combo of Ecstasy and Acid 'candy flipping' and although I didn't know why beforehand, I certainly understood it once I was there.

Without a care in the world, we rolled into the Meadowlands Stadium parking lot... obtaining a serendipitous spot that seemed prepared especially for us. After a good stretch, I broke from my group and blended in with the tie-died teddy bears as they erected swaying camps of colorful cloth using VW buses as cabins and streams. Wondering as I wandered, drinking and laughing rang through the air and every other person seemed to be strumming an acoustic guitar. A flower girl approached me and spoke to me as though she were four.

"Have you seen my friends?" she mumbled like a fading ghost.

"I don't know, why don't we look for them," I suggested as we walked.

We walked and had some light conversation that streamed in bubbles until they floated away. She spun in the opposite direction and said, "I think they're this way..." and then she was gone. I continued through the love-fest, lighter than air and grinning ear-to-ear as the summer sun beat down on my head. I'd given my straw hat to my guitar-strumming car companion who found it fetching and truly authentic. I'd simply taken my father's old straw fedora and ripped the top off it so my hair would show from the top. But he looked better in it than I did, so it was his forever. As I wandered back to my Volvo, I saw the lost flower girl had found her friends. I approached her and smiled.

"You found your friends; I knew you would" I said, with the enthusiasm of a kindergarten teacher that bordered on manic. She squinted at me like I was there to bring her back to the insane asylum. She turned away from me a bit frightened, not knowing who I was, even though I had just talked with her not more than five minutes ago.

I saw full-blown throwbacks to the Sixties. Wire-thin Jesus figures with round sun-shades and feet the color of the

Earth's various clays. Some looked as though they hadn't bathed in a decade... and they probably hadn't. Women doing whirling dervishes with naked newborn babies wrapped in slings around their necks. Golf shirt-clad teens growing beards and wearing necklaces made of hemp and beads. Frat boys and hippies, laughing as one. People looking for tickets. Rose-colored glasses and peace pipes puffing. Leather-fringed vests and hand-drawn t-shirts. Keep on Truckin' and you have some rolling papers? How ya doin' and I saw you in Detroit; Rainbow afro and eating an ice cream... putting it on his head? I got you a tape and Madison Square Garden; You went to that show and it was so cool? Not better than this and Europe 72; Shakedown street and the Mars hotel; Clipping his toenails and a patio umbrella; Purple tapestry glowing and a smoking grill; I don't eat meat and you want some chicken? This is him and who are you? I need a ticket; I need one too! We broke down in Phoenix; What was the cost? I'm broke but still going! I've been eating beans for six days straight; Snapping of cans and this is a microbrew; Fractured crystal eyes and India print poncho rug sweater shag.

My trip was just beginning... my face grinning uncontrollably. Everyone was beautiful. Passages of Hendrix floated around my mind like windblown feathers. They made more sense to me now more than ever before. Listen. There's Janis Joplin. Now I hear Hendrix again. My favorite, Axis: Bold as Love. Is that Miles Davis? Snippets of the Dead wafted over the crowd of merry pranksters. I returned to my friends who'd made a campsite of my Volvo. Ian tossed me an orange, which I devoured with child-like enthusiasm. I followed that with a cold beer, which sat in my belly and fermented into my blood. Marijuana was puffed with delight, and after an hour or two, we were ready to enter the cold, hard interiors of Giants Stadium.

Almost immediately after entering the packed stadium I lost my friends... or perhaps they lost me, I can't be sure. I pondered my ticket carefully, but the complicated numbers, sections and tiers made even less sense in my condition than they did sober. There's a feeling one gets when they come from the cement interiors of a stadium and out to the field view. It's an exhilaration that rarely wanes, even after multiple experiences. In my state, it was complete euphoria. I let the world grab my wrist and guide me to the correct seat. I gravitated towards the top, stage left and planted myself in a high spot above the standing field audience. Watching the crowd, buzzed and bouncing off one another like a mob of day glow ants, I spotted Ian and his orange sneakers, hurtling over the field wall and scrambling into the party before security could grab him.

The Dead took the stage and began plucking and hitting their instruments. The lovely sound rose up and washed over me like a cozy blanket. Suddenly I was enraptured. I understood. By God, I understood! Skeletons? Of course. Flowers? Definitely. The desert? What better place? I was thoroughly enjoying the experience. My body lost control and I shook and shimmied about without inhibition. I even danced during the bombastic drumming solo 'space.' The music got tighter, the feelings got stronger. The band had magically lifted the stadium into the air with the power of music! We were flying through the outer rings of the universe —whipping through the Milky Way and across a thousand galaxies! I was melting like butter on toast. My eyes were as wide as saucers. My pupils were catching the sparkling light of every gleaming stream of luminescence. The stars were shooting into my eyes and into my brain, firing hollow channels through me like hot coals till they exited through my feet. Then the empty channels filled with the music that vibrated through the floor, filling the channels with tingling music until it shot up and out through the ends of each strand of hair like rainbow lightning. The people around me swelled with desire. The pulse of the stadium was throbbing, palpitating, flourishing and surviving. Concrete became flesh and flesh concrete. I was contracting and receding. My head rolled back on my neck as my spine turned to jelly. The hairs on my body turned to wings, lifting me off the ground and massaging me. I smiled without thought, I thought without reason, I saw without looking and heard with feeling. My sweat turned to fruit and fed my skin as the people around me held me steady with their breath and auras. The stage was flowing, glowing, flickering, flashing, switching, on and off and left and right, purple, white, green, orange, red, purple, blue, yellow, green, purple. The set became a beast with eyes like a fly and a mind, in my mind. It controlled my desires and caused my body to respond involuntarily with the music, the light, the feeling... the feelings! The band was the beast's mouth, which spoke through the music. Each member wiggled like teeth and uttered the truth. Electricity was shooting from the amplifiers, through the air, through the currents and into every nervous system. Every twang of a guitar string, snapped like a whip, every beat of a drum rang like a thunderclap—bringing us all closer and closer. There was oneness and harmony. The crowd below me swelled like an organ, a beating heart, delivering effervescent blood, bubbling to every extremity creating efflorescence. They gushed and surged forward and back and around and around. They writhed and moaned moving through each other, around each other like satellites bouncing off the stars and planets... the Milky Way! The gods of the universe smiled down upon me. Beams of light whizzed by me like fireflies. I closed my eyes and felt the cool warm air enrapture me, transport me to the answers of all questions. I opened my eyes to see the crowd blending into one, a complete being, a field of flowers blooming, flourishing, exploding like fireworks in unison. The air grew thicker, the feelings stronger. The people, like fingers, swayed and swayed, breathing and breathing with desire, feeling and feeling. The whole crowd was holding, clutching in full throttle for a perfect explosion... when suddenly the lights went up.

    I looked down and the band was waving goodbye as they left the stage. What the hell?! I whipped my head around in confusion. I was suddenly back on Earth. "What the heck am I doing here?" I thought. My body was tingling all over. I felt like a man whose woman decided to pack her bags and leave in the middle of a love-making session. As the crowd filtered out, I found myself standing alone, staring at the stage like a kid looked over at Christmas. The stadium was nearly empty except a few vultures vacuuming the place for stoner castoff material.

    "What the hell is going on here?" I thought. "Get back here! I'm not finished up here yet!" For the first time I actually understood what it felt like to be the traveling fans who followed The Dead. Never getting enough. I imagined myself walking up to Jerry Garcia and the band, sheepishly begging for a ride. "Hey guys. You got room for one more person in that van? Hey Phil, can I be a roadie?" I felt monumentally ripped off. This couldn't have happened in the 60s, right? Didn't concerts go on for days back then? Didn't bands play until their fingers bled? Where's the encore? Is there another band? This can't be happening. This can't be happening! I needed to consort with Timothy Leary or Ken Kesey on this one. Surely, they'd have something to say about it.

  As I shuffled slowly towards the exit, I kicked a few things around and sifted through some discarded items. I found nothing of interest and certainly no answers. I entered the stadium corridors where thousands of aimless souls migrated towards the exit. I stopped and laid back on a giant industrial pipe that shot out from somewhere inside the concrete wall at an angle. I drained a bottle of water on my chest that ran down my body in vein-like streams. A girl stared at me with a look of horror. I looked at my chest... my skin melting off my bones and onto the floor. I had fused with the metal pipe I'd used for rest. The girl continued to stare unblinking... her eyes like a hungry owl. I got up and continued on with the zombie crowd.

  I squished through the industrial venue to find my friends waiting at the Volvo. I was sweating profusely like everyone else. Officially overtaken by a heat wave, there was not much else to do but ride it out. Everyone in the group thought our next adventure should include a diner that someone remembered going to once before. I, on the hand, wanted to roll around in dewy grass and make love to the soil with birds of paradise growing from the surface. People were hungry and a plastic-coated diner with buzzy fluorescent lighting seemed to be the preference. I didn't have much choice. Not only was I incapable of operating my own vehicle, if asked to point North, there was a 359 degree of chance I'd get it wrong.

At the diner, I ordered a shrimp cocktail because it seemed like the only thing that wasn't manufactured by the industrial machine that I seemed to be railing against. It went down like wet cardboard. The others noshed on bloody hamburgers... truly terrible in my condition. What the hell was going on? Wasn't everyone on the same wave I was on?

I looked out the window, waiting for a sign to lead me to another adventure. Perhaps the adventures of my hippie generation forefathers were just as disappointing as mine. Did anyone really get satisfaction? Was everyone trying to find a new thing or a new vibration? Seeking out the next best thing, a new world, a better life, the next wave, a smoother ride, a different feeling, a new sensation, a new religion? A call to all to start a New Age of Enlightenment. Write books, create art, create something that challenges everyone, scares everyone and makes everyone think. If we don't do it, no one will, and mediocrity will become the norm faster than we realize. One day we'll turn around and everything will be a wash of grey and the sound we hear will be a droning buzz as the world crumbles into a polluted sea of indifference.

Searching for signs, the only one I saw was that of a gleaming covered wagon, the logo of the dead end diner we occupied... a symbol of western movement, yet also one of travel that is slow, burdened with the stench of Dysentery and potential for a scalping. Looking into the deadened eyes of my tablemates, crushing fried potatoes with their mouth-bones, I understood that I'd be walking this journey alone. But after all, it was only a Grateful Dead concert. The swelling of my heart, and the awakened consciousness of my mind was more the result of chemistry, and not so much by six or seven guys standing on a stage thumbing metal ropes and clanking skinned tubes. If I had seen a scientist though, I'd have surely thanked them in kind.

The ride home was quiet. My car mates were pretty much exhausted and checked-out. The air rushing through the windows was a comforting source of relief from the heat. Staring out the window, I watched as the world went rushing by. Trees, cars, houses, lights... life.

I flopped down on Ian's couch and stared out the sliding glass door. In the darkness, the rippling waves of his mother's pool danced up and down in rhythmical aqua jumps. I was wired and ultra-conscious. Ian suggested a swim, so we cracked cold beers and dove in. The water was warmer than the early morning air. I floated in the deep end and stared up into space...the place I'd been only a few hours before... riding high with the fireflies and UFOs. The stars were bursting through the darkness, even as the sunrise began to bleed into the night. Ian slipped out of the water, slumped into a lounge chair and crossed into sleep. I continued to float, hoping a starship would come and take me away.

A month later Jerry Garcia was gone. He died from a long series of maladies—bad health, bad diet, bad sleep, drug addiction. I can say with confidence that the Dead show I saw that day was one of the best concerts I ever saw. Whether my mental condition played a part in it or not, I was happy to see The Dead and experience what so many people loved about the whole mystique. I got a taste of the Dead and insight to the talent of Jerry Garcia. A true genius of the guitar and a creative trailblazer that hypnotized generations of music lovers to the point where they dropped what they were doing and followed him and his band around the globe. In many ways, I still feel like I'm searching for the feeling I had that day.

After the show, I hunted down some Dead albums. My Uncle Paul gave me a stack of choice selects, and my college buddy carefully constructed some live mixes from Germany and Amsterdam. I dropped the needle on that first record, sat back and listened to the sweet sounds of Jerry's guitar as it filled the air around me.

I didn't make it past the second song. I replaced it five minutes later with Weezer, and those Grateful Dead recordings were carefully shelved, never to be touched again.

BUGGIN' OUT

15

CULT OF PERSONALITY

Early in the fall semester of my Sophomore year at Syracuse University, my buddy Fish and I decided to hitch a ride to Boston with some friends for a little weekend R&R. We'd barely clocked in a month of middling schoolwork before feeling entitled enough to take a vital respite. Fish was planning to see his girlfriend and I was going to visit my high school girlfriend Courtney who was now a Freshman at Emerson University. We sardined ourselves into the potato chip laden backseat of a hatchback with three other guys and made a beeline to Beantown.

Courtney and I hadn't really spoken since we parted for school and the lack of communication between us, mostly by me, had built an awkward tension. I know you're shocked to hear this, but men, especially 19-year-old men, tend to clam up when they're unable to properly explain their feelings... particularly about the future of relationships. When I first saw her in the street after months apart, she smiled sadly and ran into my arms. We embraced tightly with familiarity and relief. We were already different people at that point and Boston was her new town. I couldn't shake the feeling I was an uninvited guest asked to stay for dinner – the guy wedged in the corner, sitting on the folding wooden chair that's a head lower than everyone else and forced to use a red plastic plate instead of chinaware.

Within minutes of connecting with Courtney, we met up with Fish's girlfriend and soon our quartet was drinking a bottle of white wine on the Common and snacking on hummus... the first time I'd tried it. Hummus, not wine.

We all chatted happily and then parted ways. Courtney and I hoofed it to her dorm where she introduced me to a few of her friends before settling into her room, which had been vacated by her roommate for the weekend. Her room had a fantastic direct visual line to Fenway Park and the famous Citgo sign. Courtney gave me the lowdown on the ancient and supposedly haunted building she was living in. I don't remember who the main ghost was, or what their general beef was about, but I'm pretty sure it had something to do with a woman who'd been brutally butchered centuries before and not properly laid to rest. Being the only man staying on the all-female floor, I had carte blanche of the available men's room, but became prime target *numero uno* for disgruntled female poltergeists' floor-wide.

Alone in the shower, lathering away the stench of my car mates, I was immediately met with flickering lights, the shower turning hot and cold and the feeling of being, let's just say, 'not so alone.' I thought Courtney's friends were screwing with me:

"Let's tell him the dorm is haunted and flick the lights on and off while he's showering."

Yet, when the hairs on my neck sprung up like Spiderman, I tore back the plastic shower curtain with magnified intensity and found that I was most definitely alone. I bounded from the shower and skated dangerously across the slick, 150-year-old bathroom floor tiles like Brian Boitano on a gold medal day, and into the safety of Courtney's room. Needless to say, this set an ominous tone for the weekend.

Attacking Boston the next day with a bright-eyed hunger, Courtney gave me the tour. It was a stunningly beautiful day. The air was crisp and the sun was shining—not a cloud in the sky. I was clutching her hand with newfound relationship zeal and I held my head high as I took each street corner like it was the summit of a mountain. I was high on life at that moment, and that's precisely when and why it all went so horribly, horribly wrong. I was wearing my heart on my sleeve. My emotions were raw and exposed. I was feeling adventurous, like each step was a step in the right direction and I let my silly-hearted and distorted sense of discovery make a decision that my head normally wouldn't make.

We were near the seaport and while crossing the street, we saw a morose man standing on the corner holding up a crude line graph atop a brown clipboard. I'm not sure what compelled me to notice the bearded, troll-like man, but he grumbled and got my attention. I could have been drawn in by any 'lost dog' sign on a telephone pole, or a flyer for guitar lessons, or donations to free Tibet. But his argument was so compelling, I couldn't resist. With all the emotion of a mannequin, he mumbled: "Would you be interested in getting a personality rating on a graph like this?" and blandly held the graph up to my face. He spoke as if he were reading his lines off a blimp in the far-off distance.

I can't be quite sure, but I'm pretty certain my face lit up like a Christmas tree – as if I had just won the lottery. It just seemed like the most revolutionary thing I could possibly do at that moment. "Sure!" I squealed as I looked at Courtney. She, on the other hand, was not so enthusiastic. She shook her head, and mouthed the words,

"Noooooooo."

Of course, she was right, but I couldn't be denied. This guy could sell sand in the desert! I simply had to do this. Looking back, it was such a dunderheaded thing to do, but I usually chalk up bad decisions as something to experience so that I can write about later on...

The man told us to follow him, and we did. We went into a corner office building across the street, which was plush with mahogany wood and marble. I believe the place was a former bank or law office or perhaps, a slave-whipping station. But the organization was sleek and streamlined. People were working diligently like any other business. Some people were in suits and others were more casual. Some were behind desks while others were doing things just out of our view. My mind doesn't recollect, but we usually don't register everyday things like people putting papers in filing cabinets, or dissecting cats behind a water cooler. It's simple, everyday stuff. The place was buzzing with cheery, business day activity.

We were immediately placed in a conference room and asked to sit. Courtney was jumpier than a one-legged woman in an ass-kicking contest, but I was clueless. I sat in one of the many available plush chairs while our host started up an old-fashioned grade-school film projector. He mumbled, "watch this film and I'll be back in 20 minutes" and then he left.

I remember thinking that 20 minutes was kind of a long time to be stuck in this room on a beautiful day, but then my attention turned to the screen. The film was a bizarre black-and-white public service announcement, only more sanitized. Like I was watching aliens in human costumes pretending to do human things, like washing dishes or walking. And then it hit me like a ton of bricks! Whap!

WE'D BEEN CAPTURED BY THE POD PEOPLE AND THEY WERE GOING TO ANAL PROBE US AND USE OUR BODIES AS HOSTS TO COMPLETE THEIR ULTIMATE MISSION OF TAKING OVER THE EARTH!! Or something like that.

The world began closing in on me and I had an "Oh Shit" moment. You know in the movies when they yank the camera back as they pull the focus in? The background zooms out and gets all Vertigo-y and unsettling. That was me, right there. I looked at Courtney who was ready to pop.

"Let's get the hell outta here!" she pleaded.

"Yea," I said. I grabbed her hand and marched to the door.

I snagged the handle and lo and behold, the door was locked! I jiggled it again, but we were most definitely imprisoned. Then, I got a twinge of panic. I spun around and went to plan B. In complete hero mode, I jerked Courtney towards the window and yanked it open. There was a huge hedge of thick bushes in front of the window, but I was determined to get out of the building and figure out the bushes later. I stuck my leg out the window when the door opened, and the bearded man walked in.

"What are you doing?" he mumbled.

Courtney whispered a plea for us to leave, but I was already in the middle of a spiel.

"What the hell are you doing? Locking us in this room?"

He ignored my question and blurted, "Do you want to take the test now?" as robotically as he'd enticed us in the street. Now, I saw right through him… he was partially lobotomized or some kind of low-functioning drone.

I don't remember my response, but as we moved out of the room and back into the main area, I felt calmer and back in control. The main door to the entrance was wide open as the day was glorious, so it didn't seem like we were complete prisoners. We could walk out the door at any time. For some reason, I wanted to complete the mission at hand and agreed to take the test. I'm not sure why. I like to finish what I start, which is a terrible philosophy when you start really stupid activities.

The two of us were separated. I sat at a large wooden desk with a man and Courtney just to my right at a desk with a woman. You'd have thought we were taking out complicated business loans, but we were simply taking a test. A test of what, remained to be seen. The man who was administering my test was good-looking, in his 30s, with dark hair, thin and strong, with a wiry jaw and a stern stare. He slid the test in front of me and gave me a basic overview like "answer as honestly as you can" and "check off the answer that's most relevant." The test was multiple choice and had an array of bizarre scenario questions, most of which I can't remember. Nor do I really remember any of the answer choices that I had to choose from. But I do remember a few. One asked, "If you came across a burning building and realized that there were people inside, you would?" I don't recollect all the answers, but they consisted of things like "A. Run inside and save everyone, B. Call the fire department, C. Get someone else to go inside and save everyone... etc. The test took about 20 minutes.

    I don't remember if I finished the test or if it was taken from me after a certain point – S.A.T. style. Years of failing multiple-choice exams has blurred into a giant heap of stress memories. The man placed a clear Lucite sheet with a grid over the test, slid on a pair of spectacles and began to carefully look over the results. I expected him to start marking it up with a red sharpie like a schoolteacher. Most of my high school tests were returned to me looking like they'd been in a savage fencing incident and stitched up at the hospital by a one-eyed surgeon. But the administrator did nothing but simply read and read and read, his facial expression growing grimmer and grimmer until he was in full-bore disapproval. He looked up at me and dramatically pulled off his glasses. I thought he was about to tell me I'd been expelled for cheating or plagiarism. I gave him a goofy smile and said, "Well, what does it say?"

    "What does it say?" he said in disgust. "What does it say?"

    He leaned back and gathered himself, like he'd been insulted. He leaned forward, slid his jaw across his skull like he was auditioning for Tony Montana in the dinner theater version of *Scarface* and said with a hushed intensity, "It says that you are a selfish and disgusting person, that's what it says."

I blinked a few times. Then I thought for a second or two more, and blinked a few more times. Then I furrowed my brow and blurted, "What the hell did you just say?"

He responded, "It says that you are a terrible person and you need some serious help!"

"Who the hell are you to say that?!" I shot back confused.

He snatched the test, held it up and poked his finger at it aggressively.

"Your answer to the question 'If you came across a burning building and realized that there were people inside' was that you would run inside and save everyone! What are you, stupid?"

Now, I've been accused of being a bit of hothead once or twice in my life (see: always), but the rage that overtook me at that moment was volcanic. Yea, obviously it's stupid to run into a burning building, but I was 19! I would have snorted jet fuel and rollerbladed down the side of the Sears Tower at that age. I filled my lungs and screamed, "FUCK YOU!" then turned to Courtney sitting directly to my right. She was hunched over in tears – hysterically sobbing. She was paralyzed in a flood of emotion, incapable of moving. I lifted her out of the chair.

"You are a fucking asshole!" I shouted to the man, pointing at him ferociously. Then I turned to the woman that administered Courtney's test. "And fuck you too!"

Then, the escape towards the door began. It took mere seconds, but felt like a quicksand eternity. The ruckus had drawn the attention of the entire room. The people in the room, the androids or whatever they were, had all stopped and were facing us; their eyes glowing like flashlights. At least that's how I remember it. The paper filers had stopped stuffing papers into the filing cabinets and began creeping slowly towards us... like they'd been programmed to do. The cat dissectors had stopped dissecting the cats behind the water cooler and began creeping towards us... like they'd been programmed to do. Courtney and I whirled around like the last survivors of a zombie showdown. Our eyes darted about as the 15 or so humanoids moved in on us... closer, and closer still. Their frowns of disapproval magnified like ten thousand dads after a straight F report card. The light of the day grew brighter as we eased towards the exit. I made sure none of the programmed humanoids or any one of the henchmen that were assimilating a rectum in the corner, snuck up on us. I ushered Courtney calmly out, and as I was about to step out into the free air, I turned and pointed at all the people, their eyes locked in on us like the *Children of the Corn*, and shouted, "You're all a bunch of fucking assholes!" and stepped outside into sweet freedom.

    The sun hit my face and was so blinding, I had to shield my eyes. I turned back and looked inside the building entrance. Black with shadows, I saw nothing but beaming eyes peering out at us. We made it to safety to the opposite corner and peering back again, saw a few of the humanoids come into view as they stepped into the sunlight, leaned against the doorway, and watched us walk away – not dissimilar to a gaggle of crazy town folk in some backwoods community, watching the city slickers zoom out of town in their eco-friendly car after a perilously close gang raping.

Although free, I'm positive I did a few hundred over-the-shoulder looks to make sure none of the humanoids were following us. But how were we to really know? They looked just like you or me!

After consoling an emotional Courtney, we shrugged it off as best as we could and ate lunch. We walked along the water and skipped through the aquarium and spent the evening with a few friends drinking beer and recounting our wonderful adventures. Next thing I knew, I was on the T train to rendezvous in the 'burbs where I'd be shoehorned into a hatchback with four guys on a return trip to Syracuse. I listened to the new Living Colour album, *Time's Up*, over and over until we returned to our dorm. Courtney and I broke up a few days later - not because we were nearly abducted by a freakish cult with members of unknown origin, but because we were two people trying to find ourselves in the world and that was going to happen apart and not together.

Courtney and I remain good friends to this day. When I told her that I was writing about this long-since-dormant incident, she confessed that she still has flashbacks from the experience. As the years went on, I told the cult story at parties and in social situations, but after a while, I placed the story away in a hot attic spot in the corner of my mind.

I'm not sure what the organization's recruiting techniques are today, almost two decades later, but I hope they've stopped locking people in conference rooms. Maybe, they smile now. Perhaps they serve cookies or a nice ham sandwich. I would assume that whatever charming techniques they thrust on people to assimilate them into their cult, it's a bit more friendly and inviting. I sincerely doubt it though.

BUGGIN' OUT

16

FOOTLOCKER TREASURES
PART III - IN 3D

My ability to be judicious with nostalgia is unlike my grandmother Tix, God rest her soul, a notorious hoarder. I spent many summers cleaning out her garage, which would eventually turn into a series of haggling negotiations that could rival any seller in a Turkish bazaar.

"What are you doing?" she'd howl in a panic.

"Throwing out this tree branch." I'd reply, confused.

"But I'm going to paint that gold and put it in a vase." she'd say nostalgically, caressing the knotted stick to her cheek like one of her toy poodles.

"But grandma," I'd gently plead, "It's been in the garage for four years."

Her son, may father, fell short of hoarder status, mainly because of my mother, but didn't exactly throw shit away either. This is evident by his ability to produce snow shovels from thin air. I, on the other hand, have lived by the creed of the Japanese... simple design... sleek minimalism and bold colors and shapes. I am, however, a sucker for collectibles as evident by all the nooks of my office full of Lego toys, Wolverine comic books and walls covered in vintage James Bond Posters.

My once-firm stance on tossing literally everything and anything from the footlocker that reminded me of my past life, had softened like warm molding clay. Photos and love letters I'd been preparing to set ablaze, jumped back into the 'keep' pile. Plucking random letters from friends... Kevin in San Fran and my good buddy Mark Zito in San Diego, most of them are in reply to letters I sent. Over the years I thought I'd been a horrible friend and lost touch with people on my end... had been too caught up in the momentum of my craziness to keep them in my life... or just lazy.

But as I go through, I see mostly apologies for not keeping up communication on *their* end. For a brief moment I'm offended even though seconds before I'd been the terrible friend, but I realize... it's just life. It moves fast and people are constantly in and out of life. Whether you want them to be or not. They move away, they move on... they move to another country... another time zone... another dimension. Or they end up in heaven or hell... whatever you choose to believe.

Through the footlocker mire, there's some delightful gems, like sketch books I'd done in middle school when I was about 12 and 13 years old. They were innocent, but incredibly funny. Long before the jaded world took over... before a broken heart and real-world stress. Before hard decisions and forks in the road.

Flipping through these sketch book pages at random, I stop on a lumberjack chopping down a fully decorated Christmas tree. The confused lumberjack says "Oh, is this your tree?" as a shocked family looks on in disbelief. Another page, a man carries a Boombox radio on his shoulder and notices another man across the street with an entire Jukebox on his shoulder. Another page, Santa, with a hole in his head, is grumbling about giving out cannons for Christmas this year. It goes on and on.

There's a sketchbook where I drew half of it with my left hand. A book where I drew nothing but chickens. A book of people casually engaging with people with severed limbs or accidentally speared with arrows and cutlery. A book of body excrements of varying degrees, from all sorts of animals, dropping from various heights and in various sizes and viscosities. My style is already in place... a style that would stay with me until now. A sure hand and a very particular look. These books strike a chord in me. It's easy to say, "When I became a man, I put away childish things," but that person still exists inside me. The childish sensibility is pure. That 12-year-old kid cracks me up. His work is good. Sweet yet sharp. Some of it hilarious. The foundation of my sense of humor. They're quick-hit stories. One-page punchlines. Zingers and silly notions. Rapid-fire and free. I can see why advertising got into my blood. I was a natural.

A calm Sunday night. The scattered mess of ancient ephemera that once was crammed in the footlocker is now a concentrated jumble of treasures: select photos, letters and a few pieces of art and sketchbooks that all fit neatly in a small cardboard box. It was a big purge. Almost 95% of the footlocker's inner belly was tossed away. And the black mold-laced locker that was a suspected biohazard is heading to the next morning's garbage haul.

I drag the locker to the curb in the glowing dusk of a pink and powder-blue cotton candy sky, along with the construction bag remains of the filtered art materials that once resided inside and the kitchen trash that stunk like sweaty corn.

I stop and stand among the garbage pile, watching the glowing sky turn into night. The stars poke out through the cover of darkness. It's a dad thing, standing next to your trash, hands on your hip, looking out over the distant trees. Watching rolling clouds creep by, hundreds of miles beyond your little yard. Contemplating life. My dad probably did it... my grandfather too. What better place to get wistful than in the middle of rotting materials? It evokes a primitive nature in you. Cavemen didn't know what the little white dots in the dark sky were... but we do.

•••

There is a feeling I get when I think of infinite space. It's endlessness. It's vastness. It's impossibility. The fact that it never ends and how that seems impossible. Because everything has an end; Right? But the vastness of space, and in comparison, our size in relation to it all, is a feeling of smallness. It gives me a strange sense. Something I don't believe there is a word for. It could be sadness or loneliness... isolation or perhaps, inner peace. This feeling of being truly alone. Not unlike one would feel in a large open field or out on the ocean. But this loneliness expands out to the stars, the universe. So far out, that to travel the speed of light for thousands of years would get you virtually nowhere. And even if you did get somewhere, there may be nothing there. That is truly alone. And that feeling is not in the dictionary as far as I know. Perhaps there is an ancient word for it. Perhaps NASA has a term for it rolling around the hallways. Perhaps it's the feeling of floating in space... with no gravity, or time or place.

It is a feeling I get in my soul and one I treasure when I think of the vastness of space. And the perplexing thought of time, and what time is and how time actually works. Does time exist? What is time? What is aging? Is the Earth rotating around the sun actually time, or is it something else? When we age, is it because of time or is it because the body just breaks down and deteriorates? Is time just a name we gave something that is much more complex than we could ever comprehend? And the past. Is it in the past? Or is the past still happening? Is it here now? Time is just a tool. A watch is just a device to show us that the Earth has rotated and a calendar is a map to show us where the Earth is in relation to our sun. But in reality, time is not real. Time doesn't pass. Because you are now 30, or 47 or 77, doesn't mean you are no longer 15. You are. Just because the hands of your watch spun around the face a few thousand times doesn't mean your inner child is not there. It is. It's in the room with you. It never left.

When people refer to time travel, what they are alluding to is not the jumping of one time to another, it is inter-dimensional travel. Our existence is broken into dimensions. Thousands, potentially millions, and perhaps even an infinite number of alternate selves living alongside your current self in another dimension. Like a massive, never ending ice cube tray. So, to travel "Back in time," to see yourself at 15 would actually require you to cross over into another dimension. Somehow cross the barrier that separates you and your 15-year-old self. Hopping from one ice cube tray cup to another. Obviously that technology doesn't exist... this ability to open a wormhole and step into, or cross over into another dimension. It's the stuff of movies, but it doesn't mean we don't feel the pull of our former selves. Throwing something precious away is a tug on the heart, but it may actually be the longing of the person who is still there with you.

    I think about the letters and the artwork I'd tossed, and I have a tinge of regret. Regret for the fact that I was angry with it, but also regret that I threw it away. It's still mine. It's the person's that is still with me that I don't see anymore. Perhaps the person that I will be when the earth has turned a few times and I'm of the number 77 and I think about what 47 me did, I will be wistful. I will see what 47 did, what he did to 18, 26, 33 and 41 and 77 will either be angry, regretful... or will completely understand. But 77 will not be able to do anything about it. I mean, these items were of no use to the current me. But it's disappointing to the other versions of me that are still there. It sparked the memories and I moved along. But taking the journey, for lack of a better word, backwards has given me a duality. Time, if that's what you want to call it, is the most precious commodity. The older you get, the more valuable it becomes until it's priceless. Your mortality creeps in and everything changes.

    One of my favorite books is Bruce Lee's *The Tao of Jeet Kune Do*. It's a wonderful read, filled with martial arts movements and packed with life lessons and philosophies. But once you reach the end of the book, Bruce suggests throwing it away or using it as a rag as it's not useful to you anymore. I suppose it's a statement about closure and moving on. Which I can tell you is an excellent idea. To move on. Although I'm not one to use excellent literature as a paper towel. It would be better served giving it to someone else to read. But the sentiment is sound. Absorb it, learn from it... use it... and move on. You have to move forward because there's no going back. If there is even a back.

  This book might take me on a new and exciting journey. Or perhaps it will be used as a dishrag. I still want to chase my dreams. I want to try and make a full-length animated film that everyone loves. You don't get a lot of time on this planet... I've got one shot on this spinning rock and I'm not sure I'll be back. Unless you believe in reincarnation, which I don't. Even if I was reincarnated, I would probably come back as a bed bug.

  Or maybe I'd be reincarnated as a butterfly. Unfortunately butterflies only live for about two weeks once they emerge from their chrysalis transformation. I'm pretty sure that's not enough time to make a film and I don't think butterflies have the ability to use animation programs or the strength to hold a camera. But they can fly. And maybe... just maybe, floating around for a few days in the warm summer sky, is all I really wanted anyway.

BUGGIN' OUT

In loving memory of:

Charlie Spak

I'm sorry *I* wasn't the for *you*.

www.ingramcontent.com/pod-product-compliance
Lightning Source LLC
Chambersburg PA
CBHW051425290426
44109CB00016B/1443